The
Com
Acia
Drops

The Complete Acid Drops

Kenneth Williams

Introduced by
Gyles Brandreth

ORION

An Orion paperback
First published in Great Britain by Orion in 1999
This paperback edition published in 2000 by
Orion Books Ltd,
Orion House, 5 Upper St Martin's Lane,
London WC2H 9EA

A CIP catalogue record for this book is available
from the British Library.

ISBN: 0 75283 725 7

Printed and bound in Great Britain by
The Guernsey Press Co. Ltd, Guernsey, C.I.

Contents

Kenneth Williams 1926–1988 vi
Acknowledgements vii
Introduction by Gyles Brandreth viii
Preface by Kenneth Williams xv

Acrimony 3
Bitchery 8
Carping 14
Devilry 20
Epigram 25
Feuding 30
Gamesmanship 37
Humiliation 45
Invective 53
Jibing 60
Knock-out 65
Lampoon 74
Malice 80
Nemesis 85
Obloquy 91
Pique 95
Quip 103
Ridicule 111
Scorn 118
Terseness 124
Upstaging 131
Vitriol 139
Wordplay 144
Xenophobia 152
Yahoo 157
Zany 165

Kenneth Williams
1926–1988

WILLIAMS, Kenneth; actor; born 22 February 1926; died 14/15 April 1988; son of Charles George Williams and Louisa Alexandra (*née* Morgan); one sister, Pat. Educated: Lyulph Stanley School; Bolt Court, London. Formerly lithograph draughtsman. Made first appearance on stage, Victoria Theatre, Singapore, playing the detective in *Seven Keys to Baldpate*, 1946, then Ninian in *The First Mrs Fraser*, Newquay Repertory Theatre, Cornwall, 1948; first London appearance as Slightly in *Peter Pan*, 1952; Dauphin in *Saint Joan*, 1954; Elijah in Orson Welles' production of *Moby Dick*, 1955; Montgomery in *The Buccaneer*, 1955; Maxime in *Hotel Paradiso*, 1956; Kite in *The Wit to Woo*, 1957; Green in *Share My Lettuce*, 1957; Portia in *Cinderella*, 1958; *Pieces of Eight*, 1958; *One Over the Eight*, 1961; Julian in *The Private Ear and the Public Eye*, 1962; Jack in *Gentle Jack*, 1963; Truscott in *Loot*, 1965; Bernard in *The Platinum Cat*, 1965; Drinkwater in *Captain Brassbound's Conversion*, 1971; Henry in *My Fat Friend*, 1972; Barillon in *Signed and Sealed*, 1976; *The Undertaking*, 1979. Directed: *Loot*, 1980; *Entertaining Mr Sloane*, 1981. Films: *Trent's Last Case*, 1952; *The Beggar's Opera*, 1952; *The Seekers*, 1954; and twenty-five of the twenty-nine films in the *Carry On* series, from the first, *Carry On Sergeant*, 1958, to the last, *Carry On Emanuelle*, 1978. Radio: *Hancock's Half Hour, Round the Horne, Beyond Our Ken, Stop Messing About, Just A Minute*, etc. Television: *Hancock's Half Hour, International Cabaret, The Kenneth Williams Show, Jackanory, Countdown*, etc. Publications: *Acid Drops*, 1980; *Back Drops*, 1983; *Just Williams*, 1985; *I Only Have to Close My Eyes*, 1986; *The Kenneth Williams Diaries*, 1993; *The Kenneth Williams Letters*, 1996. Recreations: calligraphy, reading, music, walking.

Acknowledgements

Kenneth Williams' *Acid Drops* was conceived by Gyles Brandreth, researched by Clive Dickinson, written by Kenneth Williams, and originally published by Peter Shellard at J.M. Dent & Sons in 1980. This special complete edition contains a new introduction as well as additional material intended for the original edition but not previously published. The illustrations are by Michael ffolkes and Graeme Garden.

Introduction

by Gyles Brandreth

Acid Drops was Kenneth Williams' first book and his most successful. The idea and the title were mine, but the book – and its success – are entirely his.

In the 1970s, in my twenties, with my wife Michele Brown, I started an editorial services business, creating popular non-fiction books for publishers in Britain and America. One day, in the summer of 1979, I wrote to Kenneth, care of his agent, suggesting that he might like to lend his name to a collection of caustic quips and witty put-downs. We met; we got on well; it happened.

How it happened – the day by day process of creating the book – was extraordinary. My colleague Clive Dickinson undertook the research and editorial co-ordination. Kenneth took to Clive: 'He's a bit of a dish, where d'ya find him? Oxford, eh? Quality will out.' Over a period of several months, either Clive or I, or both us, would sit with Kenneth in a smoke-filled room (Kenneth smoked non-stop) and watch in wonder as the alchemist wrought his magic. He rejected much that we had to offer, brought his own material, demanded more research, and transmogrified our dross into his gold both by retelling all the stories his own way and by providing a linking narrative peppered with anecdote, reminiscence and personal philosophy. *Acid Drops* wasn't so much written as improvised: improvised then refined, rehearsed then re-rehearsed, and finally set down. The author performed every line of the book to us, *con brio*, using the full, fantastic range of memorable voices uniquely at his disposal.

When *Acid Drops* appeared in 1980 it was an immediate best-seller. It worked because Kenneth worked hard to make it work. He liked, trusted and respected his publisher (Peter Shellard) and the publicity director (Liz Newlands). Promoting the book, on radio, on television, in bookshops, he was indefatigable, charming, professional. He travelled the length and breadth of the British Isles; he flew to Australia; he signed copies by the thousand. He might pretend to be *blasé* about it, but he was pleased and proud to have a hit on his hands. Kenneth Williams' *Acid Drops* worked also, of course, because the book reflects both its author and the kind of stories he liked best – the kind of stories he told better than anyone.

Like almost every other child in Britain in the 1950s and 1960s I grew up with Kenneth Williams. *Hancock's Half Hour, Round the Horne, Beyond Our Ken* were my favourite radio programmes. (Weren't they yours?) As a teenager in the 1960s I revelled in the *Carry On* films and admired Kenneth's work in the theatre. In 1963, aged fifteen, I went to the first night of Robert Bolt's play *Gentle Jack*. Some were there to see Dame Edith Evans. I was definitely there to see Kenneth Williams. I first met Kenneth in 1971, at a BBC photocall on the roof of Broadcasting House, and saw him occasionally thereafter in a radio or television studio. But it was thanks to *Acid Drops* that I became a friend of Kenneth's, not a best friend, but what he liked to call 'a good chum' and, over several years, quite a close one. We collaborated on the books he wrote. We spent hundreds of hours in one another's company, shared countless meals, train journeys, trips to the cinema. He was a star and a mate. He loomed large in my life. So when, on the night of 14 April 1988, he took his own life, I felt a sense of real loss and sadness, though I wasn't surprised.

Kenneth had told me that his father had committed suicide. 'When you get to the end of your rope, tie a knot and hang on. If you can. Charlie couldn't.'

Charlie Williams was a hairdresser, with a shop in Marchmont Street, Bloomsbury. According to Kenneth, the service Charlie offered his customers was unique. He did their hair his way or not at all. 'I'm not dyeing your hair. D'you want to look like a tart? Stick to your own colour. You can't improve on nature. You ought to know that. You're old enough and ugly enough.' Perhaps not surprisingly, Charlie's business didn't prosper. In time he ran out of customers and money, and when the Inland Revenue came down on him for years of back taxes, he went bust. The shop went, the house went, and Charlie drifted into desultory retirement. He lasted a year or two and then, one night in October 1962, 'took a concoction of cleaning fluid – carbon tetrachloride – and that was that.' The inquest returned a verdict of death by misadventure.

When Kenneth died from an overdose of barbiturates ('my hoard of poison') washed down with alcohol, the coroner brought in an open verdict. But the truth is that Kenneth Williams, at 62, was at the end of his tether. The final words in the journal he kept so conscientiously for more than forty years summed it up: ' – oh – what's the bloody point?'

He was in pain ('oh, this bloody ulcer and spastic colon'), he had given up smoking (a lifelong recreation), and he was waiting to go into hospital ('how I HATE those places') for an operation he dreaded. He was frightened. And he was fed up. He knew he had painted himself into a corner. Professionally and personally, he had nowhere left to go.

That he died a burden and a disappointment to himself is so sad, and wrong, because here we are, a decade and more after his death, and he seems as potent a presence as ever. The books, the tapes, the *Carry Ons*, we buy, we listen, we watch them still. That extraordinary voice continues to resonate, one of the most distinctive English sounds of our times. If you can do it (and it's a tough one to imitate: Frankie Howerd is so much easier), there's good money to be earned in the voice-over market as a Kenneth Williams sound-alike. In the late 1990s a young actor called David Benson, who had never met Kenneth, toured the country and triumphed in the West End with a one-man show that provided an uncanny evocation of Kenneth, funny and touching, and the crowds went to it, knowing Kenneth was dead, but clearly wishing he wasn't. They loved Kenneth Williams. They would like him still to be here. 'I'm a cult,' he used to scream, eyes narrowed, nostrils flaring, 'a *cult*, d'you hear?' Well, now, perhaps he is.

Sir John Gielgud – one of the pantheon of Kenneth's heroes, along with Laurence Olivier, Noël Coward, Orson Welles and Kenneth Horne – once defined the attributes necessary to a star performer as 'energy, an athletic voice, a well-graced manner, some unusually fascinating originality of temperament; vitality, certainly, and an ability to convey an impression of beauty or ugliness as the part demands, as well as authority and a sense of style.' Kenneth had all the qualifications then, yet as the years went by the offers of work on stage and screen grew fewer and less interesting. By the end they had virtually dried up. The problem, of course, was that gradually the versatile character actor and consummate revue artiste of the 1950s and 1960s became a coarsened caricature of himself. He was frightened of failure (who isn't?) and often would say 'oh, I can't be bothered, I can't be fagged' when really he meant 'I don't want to, it might not work'. Increasingly, he fell back on the mannerisms and gags and routines he knew he could rely on, running round in ever-decreasing circles. He got less work because there was less he could do. He knew it. He knew, too, that he wasn't an easy ride. Some found him quite impossible.

Kenneth and I never fell out, but then I never crossed him. He could be sweet and sour, but when he came to my house he was only sweet. Yes, he was outrageous, waspish, wickedly funny, and often wicked simply to be funny. He would say terrible things about people, dreadful, hurtful, calumnious things, without necessarily meaning them, or, if meaning them, meaning them for the moment, or, if really meaning them, not meaning them to hurt. He would go as far as he needed – and frequently far beyond – to create an effect, to provoke a reaction, if necessary of shock, preferably of hysteria. One evening after dinner, when he already had the table in a roar, he got to his feet, spun round, dropped his trousers and his pants and cried, 'Look! Look! The *bum* – it's hanging down in pleats!'

He was funny and kind (when my father died he wrote me a wonderful letter of consolation, careful and caring) and, contrary to reputation, in my experience not in the least bit mean. He was careful with his money, but until the 1980s, his earnings had never been spectacular. The *Carry On*s were regular, but they didn't pay a fortune. 'I never got more than £5,000 for any of them. None of us did.' In 1983, when London Weekend Television offered him £10,000 for *An Audience with Kenneth Williams*, he was amazed, and thrilled. 'Ten thou for one evening of my old tat!' he gasped. I said, 'Remember Whistler's line when asked how he dared demand two hundred guineas for a painting that hadn't taken more than a day to complete?' 'Oh, yes,' purred Kenneth, ' "I don't ask it for a day's work, I ask it for the experience of a lifetime!" Yes. Yes, that's it *exactly*.'

With Kenneth, references to Whistler or Ruskin always went down well. He liked to talk about art and music and philosophy. He was self-taught and widely and well-read, he had reams of poetry by heart, and enjoyed showing off his erudition. When he was writing his auto-biography, *Just Williams*, he read it to me in draft, out loud, paragraph by paragraph, and the only time we nearly came to blows was when I forced him to leave out great chunks – pages and pages, thousands of words – about Hegel, Nietzsche, Schopenhauer. 'Oh, all right, have it your own way. If you think they want the same old rubbish, they can have it. I don't care.'

He did care, of course. When people he respected suggested he wasn't fulfilling his potential or upbraided him for excessive vulgarity, he snapped back defensively. 'Have you read *Twelfth Night*? "These be her very Cs, her Us, and her Ts, and thus does she make her great Ps." And that's the greatest poet the world has ever known. Don't talk to me about vulgarity!'

Kenneth knew he went too far too often. Once we had him to supper with the head of an Oxford college, a woman he professed himself eager to meet. He liked the idea of conversation with academics. First he charmed her, then, as the drink and the devil got to him, he appalled her with a stream of the crudest obscenities. He recognised that this outlandish behaviour drove friends away, but somehow he couldn't stop himself. One of his oldest chums was the film director John Schlesinger, who had been with Kenneth, and Stanley Baxter and Peter Nichols, in Combined Services Entertainments in the Far East in the 1940s, putting on those concert parties so brilliantly evoked in Nichols' *Privates on Parade*. John hadn't seen Kenneth for some years, so we invited them for a meal. John was apprehensive, fearing an evening of self-indulgent, self-centred queeniness. In the event, Kenneth was on his best behaviour, twinkling, nostalgic, affectionate, fun. John suggested a rematch at his house and, when it came, Kenneth was at his worst. He started loud and funny, but as the night wore on grew ever louder, more raucous and less amusing. The problem, I sensed, was that, at John's, Alan Bennett was part of the party and was so delight-ful, so gently droll, that Kenneth couldn't cope with the competition and couldn't bear himself for seeing it as competition. The evening was a flop and, I imagine, John and Kenneth, once such friends, never saw each other again.

Kenneth's very brilliance as a raconteur added to his self-loathing. 'Most good talkers, when they have run down, are miserable,' said Cyril Connolly, 'they know that they have betrayed themselves, that they have taken material which should have a life of its own to disperse it in noises upon the air.'

Kenneth, full of contradictions, was angry with himself for letting his career be reduced to the chat-show circuit, yet recognised – and relished – his own skill in the genre. After recording one of his appearances on *Parkinson* early in the evening he would come on to our house to view the transmission, providing a running commentary on his own performance. 'That's good, that's *very* good. Don't I look a dish? *Lovely* tag to that story.'

He liked a good dirty story with a proper 'tag' and admired those who could 'put them over' as he did. He picked up one of his favourites at our house, from Roddy Llewellyn, and noted it next day in his diary: 'Roddy told a story about a man going into the home of two spinsters to view a Ming vase & seeing a french letter lying on the piano stool. The old lady explained, "We found it lying in the grass on the common & it said *Place on organ to avoid infection* and we haven't got an organ so we put it on the piano & do you know we've neither of us had *any* colds this year!" He's one of the few people I've ever come across who knows how to tell a story.'

Kenneth, of course, was a natural performer, but as a person I think he was probably happiest without an audience, one to one with one of the two or three amiable, tolerant, intelligent chums (usually not from the world of entertainment) who gave him time and uncomplaining, uncomplicated companionship. Kenneth liked to be what he called 'ordinary', to spend time with 'normal families'. He loved to be with the Scottish actor Gordon Jackson and his wife Rona and their children. With the Jacksons, probably more than anywhere, he felt secure. He dedicated this book to them.

Contrary to several opinions, I don't believe Kenneth was tortured by his sexuality. He was born in 1926, forty-one years before the legalisation of homosexual acts between consenting adults. He belonged to a more discreet generation, as he said, 'before the love that dare not speak its name started shouting the odds from the rooftops'. Was he homosexual? 'Mentally yes, spiritually yes, physically no,' was his sober answer. In his cups, he would tell the tale of his exciting encounter with a young Sikh in Ceylon, in a coconut grove in Kurunegala. 'It was only fumbling, just the Barclays Bank.' Customarily, when ladies were present, he eschewed the rhyming slang and put on his Noël Coward voice to roll the word 'masturbatory' round his tongue.

He was ready to lend tacit support to the Campaign for Homosexual Equality – he told me he had been to a couple of their meetings – but he wasn't interested in 'gay rights', just 'the alleviation of suffering'. 'The sex urge is just an animal instinct,' he used to say, 'the bit left over in us from the apes. It is the human heart we should be concerned with, and its intense vulnerability.'

Kenneth was so brilliant, so gifted, so vulnerable. I felt guilty about his death because I knew that I was one (of several) of his friends who had given up on him. He was very demanding and we didn't have the time or the patience for our old chum.

Not long before he died I got a postcard from him, featuring what looked like a still from a *Carry On*, a picture of Kenneth peering into a periscope. On the card he had written: 'Are you still there?' I wasn't. And now I miss him.

It could be that you are holding this book because you miss him too. *Oh, get on with it!*

Preface

by Kenneth Williams

Most actors know the story of the avuncular vicar sitting in the railway carriage with a group of actresses off to play in the pantomime *Dick Whittington*. Proffering them his bag of acid drops he genially enquired of the girls opposite, 'Which parts do you take?' and was told, 'The cat', 'Alice' and so on. Turning to the rest he asked, 'And which one of you takes Dick?' and received the swift retort, 'We all do, dear, but not for acid drops.'

One can imagine the reverend gentleman's discomfiture. He was proffering real acid drops and was repaid with a literal one: the tart retort which puts down the pompous, the pretentious, the dishonest and, as in this instance, the innocent blunderer.

In the pages that follow, I have collected some of my favourite exchanges which can fairly be described as acid drops. The cruel *bon mot* which has its sting drawn by the laughter that ensues. It was Oscar Wilde who pointed out that no comment was in bad taste if it was *amusing* – and if for that reason alone it is worthwhile preserving these delightful examples of verbal dexterity.

Dr Johnson once said that the spoken word was like a meteor flashing across the sky and illuminating only for a while, whereas the written word was like the Northern star and remained for ever in its proper station. But to consign verbal wit to that kind of oblivion would deprive us of much that is delightfully apt and pungent. Thankfully, many involuntary responses have been recorded – Johnson after all had his Boswell – and I only wish I'd had a notebook with me on the many occasions when I met some of the fluent and funny people in my own life.

I only realised the value of a diary when I stopped using it just for recording appointments and put down some of the dialogue I'd remembered. During an evening with Noël Coward, when apropos Eleanora Duse he remarked drily, 'Dreadfully overrated', I asked in wonder, 'Did you actually see her?' and he said, 'Yes – she had this dead white make-up and the hair was drawn back into a depressing bun and the entire effect was distinctly discouraging.' I recorded this comment in my journal the next day, while the dulcet tones of that precisely modulated voice were still fresh in my memory. The nice thing about quotes is that they give us a nodding acquaintance with the originator which is often socially impressive. They also give a sagacity to the asseverations of judges who cite ancient divines and learned jurists, and our own conversation laced with 'As Haldane properly remarked' gets an appreciative nod from our collocutor. As a matter of fact, Haldane said of fragmentation, 'You can analyse a glass of water and you're left with a lot of chemical components, but nothing you can drink' – a healthy reminder that we shouldn't over-examine any saying. Obviously, watched kettles do boil. I have seen rolling stones covered in moss and a stitch in time won't always save further repairs.

When Groucho Marx, pondering which of two jobs he should take, was told, 'A bird in the hand is worth two in the bush', he joyfully repeated the phrase and then asked, 'What kind of bush?' And his namesake, Karl Marx, said, 'all ideologies are evil', which leaves us wondering what to make of the ideology that his philosophical adherents propound today. When I quoted Bulwer Lytton's 'The pen is mightier than the sword' to Marty Feldman he added reflectively, 'Yes, and considerably easier to write with', which made the entire company laugh, and if some of the entries in this book do the same its purpose will be fulfilled.

The
Complete
Acid
Drops

Acrimony

'Do you wish to hasten my last hour?'

Acrimony

The very word 'acrimony' is delicious. It conjures up memories of all the sour, pungent insults that one has either delivered or wanted to deliver at moments of extreme irritation.

I remember when I was playing in a review by Bamber Gascoigne entitled *Share My Lettuce*. Each character came on the stage identifying himself by colours; thus one would say, 'I am blue', and another, 'I am brown', and so on. As soon as the first man appeared and announced, 'I am pink', an elderly blimp in the front row called out, 'How dreadfully effeminate', and made similar denigrations with each actor's appearance. When I came on with 'I am green', he shouted, 'Oh dear, another pansy', whereupon I riposted, 'Be quiet, Madam', and he departed protesting and demanded his money back from the box office. 'I have never been so rudely addressed from a stage before,' he expostulated. The manager was unmoved and told him, 'I'm sorry, but you provoked the artist', thus proving that for once acrimony was justified. An extra thrust of the rapier overcame the bludgeoning swipe of the cosh and the effect was extremely satisfying.

There is a similar story about Ethel Barrymore playing a scene with Charles Cherry, a wonderful old character actor whose masterly performance was only marginally hampered by his being a little deaf. The curtain had been up on the scene for only a few lines, when a party of late-arrivers bustled into one of the stage boxes and, paying no regard to what was happening on stage, chatted loudly for several minutes. Miss Barrymore allowed their noise to continue until it finally became so disruptive that she stepped down to the footlights and stopped the scene by addressing the party in the box directly. 'Excuse me,' she said. 'I can hear every word you're saying, but Mr Cherry is slightly hard of hearing. I wonder if you would speak up for him?'

Of course, artists have been constantly beset with problems in the reception of their work. Poor Voltaire, who is only remembered today for that satirical gem *Candide*, spent all his life tirelessly writing plays which for the most part have fallen into obscurity and neglect. What must have been even more galling was that they were received with equal indifference during his own lifetime. On one occasion he was running through his latest masterpiece with a group of friends, prior to its opening performance, when he noticed that Montesquieu, the author of the highly successful *Persian Letters*, had fallen asleep. 'Wake him up,' exclaimed Voltaire, 'he seems to imagine that he is in the audience.'

Another eighteenth-century French writer, Boileau, can probably claim in heaven to have uttered the ultimate acid drop on his deathbed. He spoke his last words to a wretched playwright who was frantically reading his latest play to the dying critic in the hope of receiving Boileau's last words of encouragement and charity. All he got was: 'Do you wish to hasten my last hour?' And all he succeeded in doing was just that.

Since one of the primary aims of an acid drop is to establish one's own superiority, while putting down one's opponents, the pithy, pungent aphorism has always been a popular favourite with politicians and satirists. These few show the effect that can be achieved by adopting an air of universal omniscience:

'History is littered with wars that everybody knew would never happen' - *Enoch Powell*.

'I think that one possible definition of our modern culture is that it is one in which nine-tenths of our intellectuals can't read any poetry' - *Randall Jarrell*.

'Manners are especially the need of the plain. The pretty can get away with anything' - *Evelyn Waugh*.

'If God made us in His image, we have certainly returned the compliment' - *Voltaire*.

The same tone can be just as effective, when applied to individuals. Tom Stoppard blighted James Joyce with this scathing remark: 'James Joyce - an essentially private man who wished his total indifference to public notice to be universally recognised.'

The great nineteenth-century scholar Thomas Macaulay dismissed Socrates with the comment: 'The more I read him, the less I wonder that they poisoned him.'

Personal insults can be made far more telling and effective by the judicious addition of what appears to be bitterness, tinged with disappointment or hurt feeling. The Prussian Prince Galitsine said to his wife, after she had confessed to being unfaithful: 'Indeed? Well, try and restrain yourself in future, my dear.'

In a similar vein George IV was informed of Napoleon's death by a courtier who said: 'Sire, your greatest enemy is dead.'

Mistaking the man's meaning, the King replied: 'By God, is she?'

I remember hearing Gilbert Harding's wonderful reply to Mae West's manager who had asked him if he could try to sound a little sexier when he interviewed her on the radio. Harding told him:

'If, sir, I was endowed with the power of conveying unlimited sexual attraction through the potency of my voice, I would not be reduced to accepting a miserable pittance from the BBC for interviewing a faded female in a damp basement.'

Abraham Lincoln must have been one of the wittiest American Presidents of all time. There was a marvellous letter which he sent to one of his procrastinating generals which epitomised the urbane acrimony that can be attained by a man with real power:

'My dear McClellan,

If you don't want to use the army I should like to borrow it for a while.

Yours respectfully,

A. Lincoln.'

•••

When the Drury Lane Theatre burned to the ground, it destroyed Sheridan's limited wealth. Throughout the fire he sat in a coffee house across the street, watching his livelihood going up in smoke. When a friend commented on his phlegmatic behaviour, Sheridan replied: 'A man may surely be allowed to take a glass of wine by his own fireside.'

•••

Mr Justice Avory was nicknamed the Acid Drop for his unbending manner and his habit of sitting silent and impassive throughout many trials. When he did choose to speak, his manner was cold and intimidating.

'You have been convicted before, haven't you?' he asked a witness appearing before him.

The man admitted that he had. 'But it was due to the incapacity of my counsel rather than to my own fault,' he told the judge.

'It always is and you have my sincere sympathy,' replied Avory drily.

'And I deserve it,' continued the witness. 'Seeing that you were my counsel on that occasion.'

Bitchery

'And how would you know with false teeth?'

Spiteful cattiness, which is paradoxically classified as bitchery, has always been associated with the female of the species – quite erroneously. Men can be, and are, just as bitchy as women, only in their case they give it a more robustly masculine title, such as 'detraction', 'denunciation', 'mordancy' or 'caustic wit'. It is also true to say that when a woman chooses to be bitchy the result is invariably more impressive than that of her male counterpart.

Take, for example, the case of Queen Caroline, the wife of King George II. Lying on her deathbed, with her husband kneeling beside her, wringing his hands in studied grief, she urged him to marry again.

'Never,' he replied. 'I will always take mistresses.'

'That shouldn't hamper your marrying' was her tart reply.

Even our own royal family are not above an occasional regal put-down. There was an occasion when the Queen Mother and another member of the royal family were attending a garden party held in their honour, during a state visit to Australia. As the reception got under way, the two royal ladies found themselves surrounded by what seemed to be a vast mob of inquisitive Australians, all eager to get a better view. Maintaining her perfect composure and continuing to smile throughout, the Queen Mother was heard to murmur: 'Please don't touch the exhibits.'

Actresses are frequently cited as past masters (or mistresses) of the cutting rejoinder. There was a perfect illustration of this in a confrontation between Lillian Braithwaite and James Agate, the then drama critic of the *Sunday Times*. Meeting at a show business reception, James Agate approached Miss Braithwaite announcing:

'My dear Lillian, I have long wanted to tell you that in my opinion you are the second-best actress in London.'

'Thank you so much,' replied the lady. 'I shall cherish that, coming from the second-best dramatic critic.'

Beatrice Lillie frequently displayed her sharp wit away from the revue or the public stage, when the occasion demanded. She found herself at dinner one evening accosted by an envious guest, who had been eyeing her magnificent row of pearls with undisguised jealousy.

'Are they real?' the woman eventually demanded.

'Of course,' replied Miss Lillie.

Whereupon the other woman reached across, snatched the pearls and tried to bite them.

'They're not,' she jeered. 'They're cultured.'

'And how would you know,' enquired the actress, 'with false teeth?'

I've noticed that actresses who have passed their prime often indulge in derogatory remarks at the expense of ingénues in show business. Bette Davis was eating in a restaurant on one occasion when she noticed an up-and-coming starlet who was the centre of attention at another table. When the other party rose to leave, Miss Davis delivered this perfectly timed comment just as the young actress was making her triumphant exit through the door: 'There goes the good time that's had by all.'

Of Jayne Mansfield, whose bust generously exceeded forty inches, Bette Davis commented:

'Dramatic art in her opinion is knowing how to fill a sweater.'

Of course, film stars do not always get it their own way. There is the legendary exchange between Margot Asquith, second wife of the Liberal Prime Minister, and Jean Harlow at a Hollywood party. Approaching the Prime Minister's wife, Miss Harlow announced:

'Why, you must be Margot Asquith,' laying heavy stress on the T.

'No, my dear,' answered Mrs Asquith. 'The T is silent, as in Harlow.'

An equally memorable confrontation occurred between two female writers, Dorothy Parker and Clare Boothe Luce, when they met at the swing door of a hotel entrance.

'Age before beauty,' said Mrs Luce, offering to let Dorothy Parker enter first.

'And pearls before swine,' replied Miss Parker, as she passed through in front.

Greer Garson was on hand to mar a moment of triumph for Joan Crawford. As the curtain fell on the 1945 première of *Mildred Pierce*, the house erupted into wild, sustained applause which Joan Crawford received rapturously.

'None of us should be surprised,' whispered Miss Garson. 'After all, my dear, you are a tradition.'

Apart from direct rejoinders or quips, bitchery has always been a useful weapon to the observer or critic. One Dublin critic dismissed the two doyennes of the Edwardian stage with: 'Mrs Campbell played Mélisande and Mme Bernhardt Pelléas; they are both old enough to know better.'

Oscar Wilde observed of an actress who was reputed to share his own sexual propensities:

'Dear ..., she is one of Nature's gentlemen.'

The celebrated French opera singer of the eighteenth century, Sophie Arnould, held her own 'reign of terror' over the green-rooms and salons of pre-Revolutionary France. Of one unfortunate actress who was perpetually losing both work and lovers as a result of her unhappy tendency to become pregnant every year, Miss Arnould had this to say: 'She reminds me of those nations that are always extending their borders but cannot retain their conquests.'

She was even less charitable to the dancer Mlle Guimard, whose celebrated performances at the Opéra consisted almost entirely of graceful arm movements. When a colleague informed her that Mlle Guimard had been hit by a piece of falling scenery during rehearsal and had suffered a broken arm, Miss Arnould replied: 'It's a pity it wasn't her leg; then it wouldn't have interfered with her dancing.'

On another occasion when a friend commented on the stunning diamond necklace that a rival actress had been given by her wealthy lover, and pointed out that it was a shame that it was so long that it almost reached the abdomen, Sophie Arnould remarked: 'C'est qu'elle retourne vers sa source.' ('It's returning to its source.')

Mind you, Dorothy Parker could be just as trenchant in her denunciations.

'That woman can speak eighteen languages, and she can't say no in any of them' was her assessment of a notorious society flirt.

'She tells enough white lies to ice a cake' and:

'She's as tough as an ox. When she dies she'll be turned into Bovril' were the ways in which she summed up two so-called friends.

These vindictive attacks are not solely confined to women, of course. Men have been lacerated by the female tongue as much as women. Dorothy Parker, again, discussing a mutual acquaintance with a friend, was told:

'You must admit that he is always courteous to his inferiors.'

To which she enquired: 'Where does he find them?'

The French novelist Françoise Sagan, asked to define her ideal man, told the questioner: 'I like my men to behave like men – strong and foolish.'

Helen Rowland was less forgiving. 'When you see what some girls marry,' she noted, 'you realise how much they must hate working for a living.' As for the state of wedded bliss, she had this to say: 'When a girl marries she exchanges the attentions of many men for the inattention of one.'

Lady Mary Wortley Montagu, herself the victim of Alexander Pope's vitriolic satires, observed of the first Hanoverian monarch, King George I: 'In private life he would have been called an honest blockhead.'

In the married life of royalty, too, pointed criticisms are not unknown. The Duchess of Windsor once remarked on her husband's practice of invariably having a simple salad lunch on his own: 'I married the Duke for better or worse, but not for lunch.' And it reminds me of the cartoon depicting her reading a newspaper headline, 'Harewood asks Queen for permission to marry', with her remarking acidly, 'He should worry – I had to ask Baldwin.'

Carping

'A bit of a critic, eh?'

Randall Jarrell once said: 'There is something fundamentally useless about critics – what's good is good without our saying so.' And I agree with him wholeheartedly, especially with the idea that critics are useless. I also agree with Clare Boothe Luce's aphorism: 'Censorship, like charity, should begin at home; but, unlike charity, it should end there.'

So often one reads the clever words of critics which censor rather than criticise a serious work of art. I well remember the review of Robert Bolt's play *Gentle Jack* in which I played Jack. The critic wrote: 'Mr Bolt was a schoolmaster: he should now bend over and take six of the best.' That is just the kind of cheap, vulgar denigration that is totally unworthy of the subject. In this case the subject was a good one. Here was a serious Englishman addressing a moral problem of our time. Even if you are going to fall you should be allowed to fall with dignity.

On the level of sarcasm and wit, however, criticism of this category can be wonderfully malicious. The English stage has been littered with failed productions that have been given their *coups de grâce* by just such carping notices. There have been just as many on the other hand which have become outstanding successes in spite of the vindictive reviews or assessments they have received. One remembers the dismissal of Ibsen's *Ghosts* by a contemporary critic as 'an open drain'. While we may not admire them as works of artistic criticism, we can secretly relish the sheer spite and disdain couched in them.

Bernard Shaw summed up a typical play of the 1890s as: 'A tailor's advertisement making sentimental remarks to a milliner's advertisement in the middle of an upholsterer's and decorator's advertisement.'

As a music critic for some years, Shaw once attended a recital given by a well-known Italian string quartet. A fellow critic, commenting favourably on the performance, said to Shaw:

'These men have been playing together for twelve years.'

'Surely,' answered Shaw, 'we have been here longer than that.'

Groucho Marx, noted more for his shameless effrontery than his dramatic appreciation, passed judgement on a first night he was once invited to attend with: 'I didn't like the play, but then I saw it under adverse conditions – the curtain was up.'

The American magazine humorist, Robert Benchley, fired a broadside at an ill-fated production by writing: '*Perfectly Scandalous* was one of those plays in which all of the actors, unfortunately, enunciated very clearly.'

A fellow American critic and director, Walter Kerr, reviewed a similar production with this succinct statement: '*Hook and Ladder* is the sort of play that gives failures a bad name.'

Heywood Broun dismissed the opening night of one production he was invited to review in ten terse words: 'It opened at 8.40 sharp and closed at 10.40 dull.'

When he wrote of the leading man in another production, 'Mr Steyne's performance was the worst to be seen in the contemporary theatre', Geoffrey Steyne took him to court.

While both sides prepared their cases, Steyne appeared in another play, which Heywood Broun also reviewed. This time he wrote: 'Mr Steyne's performance was not up to his usual standard.'

• • •

Dorothy Parker may have anticipated similar notices when she sat through the dress rehearsal of her play *Close Harmony*. In one scene the director whispered his concern about the generously upholstered leading lady: should she have been wearing a bra?

'Good God, no', replied the author. 'At least something in the play is moving.'

• • •

Music, too, is a perfect forum for acrid criticism. Sir Thomas Beecham, who, if nothing else, never minced his words, was taking a rehearsal one cold, winter morning in the Free Trade Hall, Manchester. The intonation was awful and after suffering it for an appalling length of time, Sir Thomas tapped the stand with his baton to silence the orchestra and then said to them: 'Gentlemen, it sounds like an Eisteddfod.'

I used to be very fond of Wagner a few years ago but now I listen to him less. All that *Sturm und Drang* gets a bit oppressive as you grow older. However, Rossini, who was never too enthralled with Wagner at the best of times, said of the German composer: 'Wagner has beautiful moments but awful quarter hours.'

Noël Coward, who, like Shaw, embraced both muses of drama and music, once commented on the fairies' chorus from Rutland Boughton's *The Immortal Hour*, in which they chant the line, 'They laugh and are glad and are terrible': 'Yes,' he said, 'It's a perfect description of Ensa.'

Individual artists have always felt cutting, personal criticism far more deeply, for obvious reasons. I shudder to think how the unfortunate actress in question responded to another of Coward's urbane comments, on her own performance: 'Her Victoria made me feel that Albert had married beneath his station.'

Dorothy Parker, reviewing Katherine Hepburn's performance in a Broadway show, said: 'She ran the whole gamut of emotions from A to B.'

W. S. Gilbert deflated Sir Herbert Beerbohm Tree's *tour de force* as Hamlet with this delightfully simple comment on it: 'Funny without being vulgar.'

I have heard that Tree was also the butt of Sir Henry Irving's humour on many occasions. Irving was recruiting the services of a horse for one of his productions. After auditioning several possible animals he chose one and began to question its owner carefully about its previous stage experience.

'Has it been trained for the stage?' he enquired.

'Indeed, yes,' was the confident reply. 'In fact it recently supported Mr Tree in a play and gave every satisfaction, though I have to admit that now and again a passing flatulence did cause it to break wind.'

'Ah,' remarked Irving to the horse, 'a bit of a critic, eh?'

Only a short time after his very successful American tour of *Hamlet*, Irving heard that another production of the play was about to leave for the States, with Wilson Barrett in the lead. When Irving questioned Barrett about the wisdom of this venture, Barrett turned on him and snapped:

'You don't think you are the only actor who can play Hamlet, do you?'

'Not at all,' answered Irving, 'but you are the only actor who can't.'

In his 1888 production of *Macbeth*, Irving failed to win Oscar Wilde to his cause, in spite of taking the lead opposite Ellen Terry as Lady Macbeth. 'Judging from the banquet,' wrote Wilde, 'Lady Macbeth seems an economical housekeeper and evidently patronises local industries for her husband's clothes and the servants' liveries, but she takes care to do her own shopping in Byzantium.'

Professional criticism aside, the criticism of the public and one's fans can be terribly galling, too. A priceless illustration of this audience censure is the conversation overheard at the end of a performance of David Turner's *Semi-detached*, starring Sir Laurence Olivier. Two elderly ladies who had gone to see their idol of the great classical roles came away bewildered and disappointed after his performance as a balding, seedy and decidedly down-at-heel Midlander, so very different from his Henry V and Hamlet.

'Hasn't he gone off?' commented one of them to her companion.

'Yes, he's not the same since he married that Joan Plewbright.'

Great works of literature have not passed unscathed any more than great artists. Richard Porson, the eminent eighteenth-century classical scholar and a man of prodigious mental prowess (he could recite all of *Paradise Lost* backwards and forwards from memory – though God knows why), was in the habit of frequently quoting large chunks of Gibbon's *Decline and Fall of the Roman Empire*. In spite of his evident admiration for this work, Porson frequently observed that there could be no better exercise for a schoolboy than to turn a page of it into the English language!

Although Porson may have known *Paradise Lost* by heart, the comment of the Restoration poet and contemporary of Milton, Edmund Waller, shows that he had no intention of even trying to commit it to memory. Finding much of Milton's epic difficult to get through myself, I can easily sympathise with his view: 'If its length be not considered a merit, it hath no other.'

Lesser works have always been fair game for the literary critic of course, and the inimitable Dorothy Parker must sum up the feelings of many book reviewers when she wrote of one aspiring best-seller: 'This novel is not to be tossed lightly aside, but to be hurled with great force.'

Devilry

Union of political thieves

One of the greatest values of humour is that it provides us with a safety-valve. If you think of all the naughty and unkind thoughts that you have harboured against other people, or life in general, it is always a tremendous relief when you find that someone has actually had the temerity or courage to give voice to them. More often than not we protect ourselves by labelling this brave soul 'a cynic', but secretly we relish his carping denunciations with a vicarious delight, tempered only by our own timidity.

• • •

Even among the acknowledged aficionados of the *bon mot* and the social diatribe, there are some who have shied away from the true significance of cynicism. 'A cynic is a man who knows the price of everything and the value of nothing,' said Oscar Wilde; while in a similar tone H. L. Mencken defined a cynic as 'a man who, when he smells flowers, looks around for a coffin'.

• • •

However, braver hearts have succinctly encapsulated the importance that cynicism holds for all of us, but which we seldom admit, even to ourselves.

'The power of accurate observation is commonly called cynicism by those who have not got it,' said wise Bernard Shaw, cutting through the myopic haze of self-delusion. And from across the Atlantic comes Lillian Hellman's matter-of-fact analysis: 'Cynicism is an unpleasant way of saying the truth.'

No doubt to the chagrin of many of the foremost British wits, the greatest single hymn to cynicism was written by an American. Oscar Wilde, Bernard Shaw and Max Beerbohm were all at the height of their sardonic careers when Ambrose Bierce was compiling his wickedly trenchant and telling *Devil's Dictionary*.

Addressed to enlightened souls who prefer dry wines to sweet, sense to sentiment and wit to humour, the *Devil's Dictionary* is a crucible of vintage invective and malice.

This is a selection from Bierce's work offered in homage to the man who glossed 'a cynic' as: 'A blackguard whose faulty vision sees things as they are, not as they ought to be.'

Acquaintance: A person whom we know well enough to borrow from, but not well enough to lend to.

Alliance: In international politics, the union of two thieves who have their hands so deeply inserted in each other's pockets that they cannot separately plunder a third.

Bigot: One who is obstinately and zealously attached to an opinion that you do not entertain.

Bore: A person who talks when you wish him to listen.

Clergyman: A man who undertakes the management of our spiritual affairs as a method of bettering his temporal ones.

Connoisseur: A specialist who knows everything about something and nothing about anything else.

Degradation: One of the stages of moral and social progress from private station to political preferment.

Duty: That which sternly impels us in the direction of profit, along the line of desire.

Economy: Purchasing the barrel of whisky that you do not need for the price of the cow that you cannot afford.

Excess: In morale, an indulgence that enforces by appropriate penalties the law of moderation.

Fidelity: A virtue peculiar to those who are about to be betrayed.

Friendship: A ship big enough to carry two in fair weather, but only one in foul.

Glutton: A person who escapes the evils of moderation by committing dyspepsia.

Grammar: A system of pitfalls thoughtfully prepared for the feet of the self-made man, along the path by which he advances to distinction.

Hatred: A sentiment appropriate to the occasion of another's superiority.

Heaven: A place where the wicked cease from troubling you with talk of their personal affairs, and the good listen with attention while you expound your own.

Ignoramus: A person unacquainted with certain kinds of knowledge familiar to yourself, and having certain other kinds that you know nothing about.

Intimacy: A relation into which fools are providentially drawn for their mutual destruction.

Jealous: Unduly concerned about the preservation of that which can be lost only if not worth keeping.

Jury: A number of persons appointed by a court to assist the attorneys in preventing law from degenerating into justice.

Kleptomaniac: A rich thief.

Koran: A book which the Mohammedans foolishly believe to have been written by divine inspiration, but which Christians know to be a wicked imposture, contradictory to the Holy Scriptures.

Lawyer: One skilled in circumvention of the law.

Logic: The art of thinking and reasoning in strict accordance with the limitations and incapacities of human misunderstanding.

Meekness: Uncommon patience in planning a revenge that is worth while.

Misfortune: The kind of fortune that never misses.

Nominee: A modest gentleman shrinking from the distinction of private life and diligently seeking the honourable obscurity of public office.

Novel: A short story padded.

Opposition: In politics the party that prevents the Government from running amuck by hamstringing it.

Optimist: A proponent of the doctrine that black is white.

Passport: A document treacherously inflicted upon a citizen going abroad, exposing him as an alien and pointing him out for special reprobation and outrage.

Peace: In international affairs, a period of cheating between two periods of fighting.

Quantity: A good substitute for quality when you are hungry.

Quorum: A sufficient number of members of a deliberative body to have their own way and their own way of having it.

Rational: Devoid of all delusions save those of observation, experience and reflection.

Religion: A daughter of Hope and Fear, explaining to Ignorance the nature of the Unknowable.

Selfish: Devoid of consideration for the selfishness of others.

Success: The one unpardonable sin against one's fellows.

Take: To acquire, frequently by force but preferably by stealth.

Truth: An ingenious compound of desirability and appearance.

Ugliness: A gift of the gods to certain women, entailing virtue without humility.

Ultimatum: In diplomacy, a last demand before resorting to concessions.

Vituperation: Satire, as understood by dunces and all such as suffer from an impediment in their wit.

Vote: The instrument and symbol of a freeman's power to make a fool of himself and a wreck of his country.

Wedding: A ceremony at which two persons undertake to become one, one undertakes to become nothing and nothing undertakes to become supportable.

Woman: An animal usually living in the vicinity of Man, and having a rudimentary susceptibility to domestication.

Year: A period of three hundred and sixty-five disappointments.

Yesterday: The infancy of youth, the youth of manhood, the entire past of age.

Zeal: A certain nervous disorder afflicting the young and inexperienced.

Zenith: A point in the heavens directly overhead to a standing man or a growing cabbage.

Epigram

'Often it does seem a pity that Noah and
his party didn't miss the boat'

Epigram

One of the hall-marks of the genuine wit is his development of the art of the epigram. Succinct axiomatic pronouncements and detractions have always been regarded as the province of the truly accomplished satirist. Like Muhammad Ali's boxing, the epigram should be refined, elegant and pungent; in his own immortal words it should 'float like a butterfly, sting like a bee'.

This selection, arranged loosely in alphabetical order, is presented as testimony to the eternal truth that 'Brevity is the soul of wit' and, as Alexander Pope has it,

'True wit is nature to advantage dress'd
What oft was thought, but ne'er so well express'd.'

Acting: 'The art of acting consists of keeping people from coughing' – *Sir Ralph Richardson.*

Actors: 'Actors should be treated like cattle' – *Alfred Hitchcock.*

Art: 'There are two ways of disliking art. One is to dislike it and the other is to like it rationally' – *Oscar Wilde.*

Bores: 'Everybody is somebody's bore' – *Edith Sitwell.*

Consistency: 'Consistency is the last refuge of the unimaginative' – *Oscar Wilde.*

Dogmatism: 'Dogmaticism is "puppyism" come to maturity' – *Douglas Jerrold.*

Drama: 'Drama is life with the dull bits cut out' – *Alfred Hitchcock.*

Duty: 'When a stupid man is doing something that he is ashamed of, he always declares that it is his duty' – *George Bernard Shaw.*

Education: 'In the first place, God made idiots; this was for practice; then he made school boards' – *Mark Twain.*

English: 'The English may not like music, but they absolutely love the noise it makes' – *Sir Thomas Beecham.*

Experience: 'Experience is a question of instinct about life' – *Oscar Wilde.*

Fan club: 'A fan club is a group of people who tell an actor he's not alone in the way he feels about himself' – *Jack Carson.*

Fleas: 'Fleas can be taught nearly anything that a Congressman can' – *Mark Twain.*

Genocide: 'A single death is a tragedy, a million deaths is a statistic' – *Joseph Stalin.*

• • •

Home: 'The best way to keep children at home is to make the home atmosphere pleasant – and let the air out of the tyres' – *Dorothy Parker.*

• • •

Humanity: 'Such is the human race. Often it does seem a pity that Noah and his party didn't miss the boat' – *Mark Twain.*

Humour: 'Humour is emotional chaos remembered in tranquillity' – *James Thurber.*

Husbands: 'A husband is what is left of the lover after the nerve has been extracted' – *Helen Rowland.*

Idealism: 'Idealism increases in direct proportion to one's distance from the problem' – *John Galsworthy.*

Immortality: 'I don't want to achieve immortality through my work, I want to achieve it through not dying' – *Woody Allen.*

Judgement: 'It is only shallow people who do not judge by appearances' – *Oscar Wilde.*

Knowledge: 'The first step to knowledge is to know that we are ignorant' – *Lord David Cecil.*

Labour: 'Labour in a white skin cannot be free as long as labour in a black skin is branded' – *Karl Marx.*

Leisure: 'A perpetual holiday is a good working definition of hell' – *Bernard Shaw*.

Man: 'Man is the only animal that blushes. Or needs to' – *Mark Twain*.

Marriage: 'What God hath joined together no man shall ever put asunder: God will take care of that' – *Bernard Shaw*.

Modernity: 'Nothing is so dangerous as being too modern – one is apt to grow old-fashioned quite suddenly' – *Oscar Wilde*.

Morality: 'In my day, men were content with ten commandments and one wife. Now the situation is reversed' – *Saki*.

Music: 'Hell is full of musical amateurs. Music is the brandy of the damned' – *Bernard Shaw*.

Musicologists: 'A musicologist is a man who can read music but can't hear it' – *Sir Thomas Beecham*.

Nonsense: 'Good sense about trivialities is better than nonsense about things that matter' – *Max Beerbohm*.

Obligation: 'When some men discharge an obligation, you can hear the discharge for miles around' – *Mark Twain*.

Patriotism: 'Patriotism is the virtue of the vicious' – *Oscar Wilde*.

Politicians: 'An honest politician is one who when bought stays bought' – *Simon Cameron*.

Psychiatrists: 'A psychiatrist is a man who goes to the Folies Bergère and looks at the audience' – *Dr Mervyn Stockwood*.

Punctuality: 'Punctuality is the thief of time' – *Oscar Wilde*.

Quotations: 'You could compile the worst book in the world entirely out of selected passages from the best writers in the world' – *G. K. Chesterton*.

Reciprocity: 'Do not do unto others as you would that they should do unto you. Their tastes may not be the same' – *Bernard Shaw*.

Scandal: 'Scandal is gossip made tedious by morality' – *Oscar Wilde*.

Taciturnity: 'If you don't say anything, you won't be called upon to repeat it' – *Calvin Coolidge*.

Unhappiness: 'Unhappiness is best defined as the difference between our talents and our expectations' – *Edward de Bono*.

Virtue: 'Virtue is insufficient temptation' – *Bernard Shaw*.

Welfare: 'The Welfare State may be the Farewell State' – *Nancy Astor*.

Women: 'A woman's place is in the wrong' – *James Thurber*.

Youth: 'The young have aspirations that never come to pass, the old have reminiscences of what never happened' – *Saki*.

In this last quotation I think the fourth word should be 'ideals', because only ideals can never come to pass in human terms, while aspirations can be and often are realised. The ideal must forever elude mankind and all modern exhortations to healthful living will not alter the process one iota. Our birth certificates should bear the warning, 'Life is about dying', but like the cautionary instruction on the cigarette packet, it would be just as much ignored. Awareness of the ephemeral nature of humanity is something few of us seem to possess. Johnson pointed out that the imminence of death was a salutary experience for any man: 'It concentrates his mind wonderfully.' But Johnson was fortified by faith, and even Voltaire, in his atheism, was prepared to consider the possibility of meeting his Maker: 'God will pardon me – it is his business.' But then neither of these gentlemen would have entertained the notion of idealism; they both knew that of necessity the 'ideal' presupposes purity, and man is inherently impure.

Nevertheless, it is at once paradoxical and comforting to know that men do entertain the idea of perfectibility, and when the thinking man errs his qualms are voiced: guilt is the yardstick of conscience. When we say to ourselves, 'That wasn't well done', we mean we might have done it better, and resolve to try again. 'Nothing straight,' as Butler reminds us, 'was ever made out of the crooked timber of humanity.' And yet, Man will always cling to his dreams. However lowly his condition he can still aspire. Oscar Wilde expresses it beautifully: 'We are all in the gutter, but some of us are looking at the stars.'

Feuding

'If Mr Gladstone were rescued it would be a calamity'

I have always found that personal feuds and political vendettas are rich and fertile territories for the sharp-witted and sharp-tongued. In political life in particular, the raillery and banter of everyday existence are no match for the venom of the debating chamber or the stinging ripostes of a bitter opponent.

In my opinion that wonderful showman Benjamin Disraeli stands supreme among the political wits of the nineteenth century, and supreme among his opponents was the Whig leader William Ewart Gladstone. When he was once asked the difference between 'misfortune' and 'calamity', Disraeli offered this virulent definition: 'Well, if Mr Gladstone fell into the Thames, it would be a misfortune: but, if someone pulled him out, it would be a calamity.'

He was no more tolerant of the radical from Rochdale, John Bright. A colleague was telling Disraeli on one occasion of Bright's eloquence and erudition. Remarking on Bright's humble Quaker background he pointed out to the Tory leader that Bright was an entirely self-made man: 'I know he is,' answered Disraeli, 'and he adores his maker.'

Sir Winston Churchill, whose oratory thrilled me during the war, was invariably as critical of his own political opponents. Discussing the merits and failings of the Labour leader, Clement Attlee, a colleague said to him:

'At least you'll have to admit that he's very modest.'

'Absolutely true,' agreed Churchill, 'but then he does have a lot to be modest about.'

Asked for his opinion of the Labour Party as a whole, Churchill said: 'They are not fit to manage a whelk-stall.'

Even fellow Tories were not spared the occasional Churchillian put-down. Sir William Joynson-Hicks, who was successively Postmaster-General, Minister of Health and Home Secretary in the 1920s, was speaking to the Commons one day when he noticed Churchill vigorously shaking his head.

'I see that my right honourable friend is shaking his head,' said Joynson-Hicks. 'I wish to remind him that I am only expressing my own opinion.'

'And I wish to remind the speaker that I am only shaking my own head,' answered Churchill.

He was also notorious for his feuds with some of the leading women MPs. There is the celebrated exchange with Lady Astor which has been attributed to venues as disparate as the state dining-room of Blenheim Palace and the cafeteria in the Palace of Westminster. But whatever the locality the two MPs were in the midst of one of their not infrequent rows.

'If you were my husband, I'd poison your coffee,' said Lady Astor.

To which Churchill replied: 'If you were my wife, I'd drink it.'

A similar clash occurred with the Liverpool MP, Bessie Braddock, who, under much the same circumstances as Nancy Astor, exclaimed:

'Winston, you're drunk.'

'Bessie, you're ugly,' replied Churchill, 'but tomorrow, I shall be sober.'

Aneurin Bevan, a consistent adversary of Churchill's, said of one of his speeches: 'The mediocrity of his thinking is concealed only by the majesty of his language.'

Like all men in public life Churchill had his enemies outside his immediate professional circle. When *Saint Joan* was presented in London for the first time, Shaw sent him two tickets for the first night. Enclosed with the tickets was a brief note saying: 'One for yourself and one for a friend, if you have one.' Churchill returned the tickets, saying that he would be unable to attend, but adding that he wouldn't mind tickets for the second night, 'if there is one.'

Just occasionally total strangers got the better of Shaw, one of them being a country parson who had written asking for the great man's recipe for brewing coffee; Shaw, he had heard, was something of an expert. Shaw sent him what he had asked for, though he couldn't resist adding a postscript that he hoped his correspondent wasn't simply using his request as a ploy for getting his autograph. A couple of days later the post brought the clergyman's letter of thanks together with Shaw's signature carefully cut from his letter.

'I wrote in good faith,' read the letter, 'so allow me to return what it is obvious you infinitely prize, but which is of no value to me, your autograph.'

Shaw, of course, was not unaccustomed to receiving letters of this type. Sir Arthur Wing Pinero once concluded a letter to his fellow playwright with the words: 'Yours, with admiration and detestation.'

In fact the stage at that period seemed to be the setting for perpetual pitched battles or incidental skirmishes between the leading figures of the dramatic world. Mrs Patrick Campbell, Shaw's leading lady in *Pygmalion*, enjoyed a relationship with the producer, Charles Froham, which even at the best of times could only be described as 'tense'. During one of their rows, in New York, Mrs Patrick Campbell ended her tirade:

'Always remember, Mr Froham, that I am an artist.'

To which he replied, 'Your secret is safe with me.'

•••

Shaw's leading man in *Pygmalion*, Sir Herbert
Beerbohm Tree, aroused the wrath of
many adversaries. One of these was
W. S. Gilbert. Holding forth to a
friend on the popular controversy
as to whether Bacon or
Shakespeare had written
the latter's plays, Gilbert
suggested this novel solution:
    'They are going to dig up
Shakespeare and dig up Bacon;
they are going to set their
coffins side by side, and they are
going to get Tree to recite *Hamlet*
to them. And the one who turns in
his coffin will be the author of the play.'

•••

In the world of music during my lifetime, Sir Thomas Beecham and Sir
Malcolm Sargent have been the two chief antagonists, although ironi-
cally they shared the same birthday. As might be expected Beecham
was the originator of most of the famous derogatory comments. He
used to refer to the BBC Symphony Orchestra as 'Sargent's Mess' and,
throughout their long association, seldom lost the opportunity to take a
swipe at his younger colleague. When a friend was commenting in
1947 on Sargent's inclusion in the recently published Honours List,
Beecham remarked: 'I didn't know that he'd been knighted. It was only
yesterday he was doctored.'

Sargent was once conducting in Tel Aviv during a period of great
civil unrest. Palestinian terrorists had been attacking all the principal
cities in Israel during the preceding weeks, and it came as no surprise
when the performance was interrupted by the sound of gunfire directed

at the concert hall. When the news of the attack reached Beecham his only comment was: 'I had not realised that the Arabs were so musical.'

One of the most damning of his many put-downs was his description of Herbert von Karajan as: 'A kind of musical Malcolm Sargent.'

The battle of the sexes also takes on an extra dimension in the artistic world. Sparks flew the first time that Spencer Tracy met Katharine Hepburn. They were about to make a film and had been brought together for an informal meeting before they actually started work. Greeting her leading man, Miss Hepburn remarked icily:

'I'm afraid that I'm a little tall for you, Mr Tracy.'

'Not to worry, Miss Hepburn,' he replied. 'I'll soon cut you down to size.'

Some of the great satirists of history have handled their domestic troubles with the same caustic wit that has characterised their public writings. John Dryden preferred to spend considerably more time with his books than with his wife, Lady Elizabeth, a fact that did not escape her attention. Complaining to her husband about his neglect one day, she told him:

'Lord, Mr Dryden, how can you always be poring over those musty books? I wish I were a book, and then I should have more of your company.'

'Pray, my dear,' answered the poet, 'if you do become a book let it be an almanack, for then I shall change you every year.'

In the academic world, too, private feuds have often taken the form of great public expositions of wit and malice. The late Sir Maurice Bowra said of the physically unprepossessing writer, Cyril Connolly: 'He's not nearly as nice as he looks.' And he would frequently introduce younger colleagues for whom he held no great respect: 'He's a coming man: hasn't come yet.'

Richard Porson, who, like Bowra, was a larger-than-life figure, probably had as many enemies as Regius Professor of Greek at Cambridge during the eighteenth century as Bowra had while Warden of Wadham and Vice-Chancellor of Oxford one hundred and fifty years later. Porson was discussing Greek poetry with John Gillies, a leading Greek historian, when Gillies remarked emphatically:

'We know nothing of the Greek metres.'

To which Porson replied: 'If, Doctor, you will put your observation in the singular number, I believe it will be very accurate.'

The animosity felt towards Porson by his peers is evident in the infuriated remark by one fellow to him:

'Dr Porson, my opinion of you is most contemptible.'

'Sir,' replied Porson, 'I never knew an opinion of yours that was not contemptible.'

Benjamin Jowett, another eminent classical scholar and a famous nineteenth-century Master of Balliol, was frequently subjected to malevolent onslaughts from his rivals. During the period in which Jowett was working on his masterly edition of Plato, C. S. Calverley, the equally talented parodist, got the better of him while guiding a party of visiting Americans around Oxford one afternoon. When they came to Broad Street, Calverley stopped his party outside the Master's lodgings of Balliol:

'This, ladies and gentlemen,' he announced, 'is Balliol College, reckoned to be the second oldest college in Oxford. The head of this college is the Master. The present Master is the celebrated Professor Jowett. That is Professor Jowett's study.' Then, picking up a handful of gravel he tossed it at the bay window above him. Red-faced and furious, Jowett appeared at the window:

'And that, ladies and gentlemen, is Professor Jowett.'

Gamesmanship

'Don't sell so much froth'

Gamesmanship

I think the analogy between witty repartee and fencing is a good one. In the cut-and-thrust of vicious verbal exchanges, the real experts delight in their skill at parrying the leaden blows of their heavy-handed opponents. Turning these lunges aside with effortless panache, they leave their assailants floundering and defeated by their own overbearing clumsiness. It is the same matchless virtuosity which distinguishes the champion angler playing his catch, or the judo black-belt throwing his opponent, from their aspiring rivals. It is gamesmanship pure and simple.

Not surprisingly, many of these encounters have taken place in the world of politics, both in the debating chamber and at the hustings. I remember being taken by my father to listen to Aneurin Bevan speaking in St Pancras Town Hall. Bevan was well into his speech when a man sitting almost next to us started shouting:

'We don't want Labour and we don't want the Conservatives, why can't we have the Liberals?'

There was a pause and then Bevan said: 'Yes, I was never one to frown upon ambition.'

• • •

Richard Brinsley Sheridan, the famous eighteenth-century playwright and later one of the leading politicians at the end of the century, developed a reputation as the most dazzling parliamentary speaker as well. The average, run-of-the-mill MPs, drawn from among the ranks of the landed gentry, were no match for the author of *The Rivals* and *The School for Scandal*. During the course of one heated debate, Sheridan led his intended victim into a delightful verbal trap through his denunciation of another:

'Where, oh where,' he asked the House, 'shall we find a more foolish knave or a more knavish fool than this?' At which the unfortunate MP burst out with:

'Hear, hear!'

•••

Sheridan's fellow politician, John Wilkes, was campaigning for election to one of the parliamentary seats in Middlesex, when he was informed by a heckler:

'I would rather vote for the devil than for John Wilkes.'

'And if your friend is not standing?' asked Wilkes in reply.

Benjamin Disraeli was as eloquent and cutting in his off-the-cuff retorts as he was in his parliamentary set-pieces. Shouted at by one heckler:

'Speak up! I can't hear you', Disraeli answered:

'Truth travels slowly, but it will reach you in time.'

On the other hand he could turn the tables on his more adroit political rivals with equal style and wit during his speeches. He once delivered this perfect parody of Gladstone's oratory, describing the Whig leader as:

'A sophisticated rhetorician, inebriated with the exuberance of his own verbosity, and gifted with an egotistical imagination that can at all times command interminable and inconsistent series of arguments, malign an opponent and glorify himself.'

(But perhaps my favourite remark of Disraeli's came at a dinner where all the food arrived cold in a room already freezing. He commented mournfully, 'Well, at least the champagne's warm.')

Lady Astor, the first woman to sit in either of the Houses of Parliament, was a constant target for hecklers throughout her political career.

During her first campaign in Plymouth a mother shouted to her at one meeting:

'My children are as good as yours.'

To which she instantly replied: 'As which of mine? I've got some worse than any of yours – but I might have one who was better.'

At another meeting a man called out:

'Your husband's a millionaire, ain't he?'

'I should certainly hope so, that's why I married him.'

(She would have smiled at Clare Boothe Luce's comment, 'In politics, women type the letters, lick the stamps, distribute the pamphlets and get out the vote. Men get elected.')

Lady Astor's sense of style is not unknown in the Upper Chamber. Lord Mancroft silenced one persistent heckler who had a very loud voice, thus: 'A man with your intelligence should have a voice to match.'

In the world of international affairs the combination of statesman-like aplomb and British sang-froid has vanquished many powerful adversaries. Harold Macmillan is a shining example of these virtues. During the period of the 'Cold War' he was addressing the Security Council of the United Nations. Seated opposite him was the Russian Premier, Nikita Khrushchev. At one point in Macmillan's speech Khrushchev disagreed so vehemently with what he had said that he took off one of his shoes and banged the heel on the table in protest. Unmoved by this outburst, Macmillan turned to the interpreters and asked: 'I wonder if I might have a translation?'

During one of his election campaigns the Australian Premier, Sir Robert Menzies, was speaking at a local meeting when a heckler called out, 'I wouldn't vote for you if you were the Archangel Gabriel.'

'If I were the Archangel Gabriel,' Menzies replied, 'you would scarcely be in my constituency.'

Gamesmanship is by no means restricted to politics, however. It can be used to establish insurmountable superiority over rivals or associates in any walk of life. Its artful manipulation can deflate the pompous, silence the ignorant and trap the unwary. While throwing others off their guard the practitioner of gamesmanship invariably takes command of any situation and exploits it with devastating consequences.

• • •

The early nineteenth-century poet, Thomas Campbell, achieved a stylish volte-face by this means at the height of the Napoleonic wars. He was a guest at a literary dinner, at which most of the diners were impoverished writers of one sort or another. As the port was being passed round after the meal he asked leave to propose a toast. This granted, he rose to his feet and to the horror of his hosts proceeded to give the health of Napoleon Bonaparte. For a moment the company was struck dumb in appalled silence. Then angry voices rose in a crescendo of reproof and cries of outraged patriotism, till Campbell said:

'Gentlemen, you must not mistake me. I admit that the French Emperor is a tyrant, I admit that he is a monster, I admit that he is a sworn foe to your nation, and, if you will, of the whole human race. But, gentlemen, let us be fair to our great enemy. We must not forget that he once shot a bookseller!'

• • •

Dr Samuel Parr, a leading eighteenth-century Latinist, who rejoiced in being referred to as 'the Whig Johnson', was completely hoodwinked in this way by the Lord Mayor of Oxford, one Harvey Combe. Dr Parr had been invited by the mayor to deliver the Spital sermon in Christ Church Cathedral. After the service they were leaving together and Parr asked Combe:

'Well, how did you like the sermon?'

'Why, Doctor,' replied the mayor, 'there were four things in it that I did not like to hear.'

'State them, then.'

'Why, to speak frankly then, they were the quarters of the church clock, which struck four times before you finished.'

John Wilmot, the second Earl of Rochester, was a notorious Restoration libertine and rake, who epitomised the satirical wit that pervaded the court of Charles II. As the 'enfant terrible' of high society, Rochester knew no bounds for his scathing attacks, and even the King did not escape the venom of his tongue or his pen.

'Here lies a great and mighty king
Whose promise none relies on:
He never said a foolish thing,
And never did a wise one.'

This was the Earl's epitaph on his sovereign, written while Charles was still alive. However, the King succeeded in turning the tables on the wayward peer with this response: 'This is very true: for my words are my own, and my actions are my ministers'.'

On another occasion Rochester unexpectedly met his match in the mathematician and theologian, Isaac Barrow. Encountering the bookish priest at court one day, Rochester saluted him:

'Doctor, I am yours to my shoe tie.'

Realising his aim, Barrow returned his address with:

'My Lord, I am yours to the ground.'

Improving his blow, Rochester answered:

'Doctor, I am yours to the centre,' which was countered with:

'My Lord, I am yours to the Antipodes.'

Refusing to be fooled by what he referred to as a 'musty old piece of divinity', Rochester exclaimed:

'Doctor, I am yours to the lowest pit of hell.'

'And there, my Lord, I leave you,' said Barrow, with devastating finality.

Another member of the cloth, Archbishop Roberts, put a young interviewer smartly in his place on his correct style of address:

'Your Grace – or Father?' said the young man. 'I believe you prefer to be called Father?'

'Same as God, yes: Father.'

James McNeill Whistler could be as disarmingly frank at times. He once enquired of a publican:

'My man, would you like to sell a great deal more beer than you do?'

'Aye, sir, that I would.'

'Then don't sell so much froth.'

Whistler's contemporary and associate, Oscar Wilde, had a similar line with shopkeepers. Entering a florist's one day he asked:

'Can you take flowers out of the window?'

'Certainly, sir, which would you like?'

'Oh, I don't want any. I only thought some of them looked rather tired.'

Bernard Shaw adopted a similar technique with a heckler on the opening night of *Arms and the Man*. At the end of the performance there was tumultuous applause. Shaw appeared on the stage and good-humouredly accepted the audience's raptures. One of them was not at all impressed by the new work, however, and he began to express his disapproval by shouting 'Rubbish' at the top of his voice. Hearing the dissident's voice above the hubbub, Shaw shouted back: 'I agree with you, my friend, but who are we two against the hundreds here who think otherwise?'

Sir Thomas Beecham seldom missed an opportunity to score points against his professional colleagues. He was rehearsing a new work by Delius one day, with the composer sitting in the auditorium.

'Was that all right, Fred?' asked Beecham at a convenient break in the score.

'Yes, except for the horns, perhaps,' was the reply.

'Gentlemen, we'll try from bar six again,' Beecham told the orchestra.

'Yes, that was all right,' said Delius when they had finished.

'Oh good,' Beecham replied. 'You know there are no horns in that passage.'

Perhaps the final word should go to Stephen Potter, the inventor of gamesmanship, sportsmanship and one-upmanship. He once described an 1897 port which had long since passed its prime in this way: 'The imperial decay of the invalid port ... its gracious withdrawal from perfection ... keeping a hint of former majesty, withal ... whilst it hovered between oblivion and the divine *Untergang* of infinite recession.'

Very eloquent, but I don't need that to put *me* off port. I haven't touched a drop since I spilled a decanter of it over a film producer at the Mirabelle. The Stilton was consumed amid the aroma of wet wool and vintage Cockburn's. And it came as no surprise when the Hollywood contract didn't materialise.

Humiliation

'Oh I've often helped daddy when he was much drunker than you'

Humiliation

I was dining in a restaurant with a friend who had chosen a place with booths, because he said the sound did not travel. I was sitting there not being terribly theatrical (my friend was nothing to do with the theatre anyway), while across the gangway there were two other men having a furious argument. Finally one of them rose and said in very distraught voice:

'I can't stand any more of this,' and rushed out of the restaurant.

The other called after him: 'Come back, I haven't finished my sweet.'

But his friend had gone. He looked round the room and saw me. Not having shown any interest until then, he suddenly said:

'Oh, it's you! Hm, you're almost as bad off as you are on. Thank you for a *great* disappointment.'

The manager rushed over to apologise and explained that he was usually a most courteous customer but that he'd obviously had too much to drink. I said:

'Not at all. Such loquacity is to be welcomed in a world of gross mundanity.'

'You are very kind,' he replied. 'Please accept this meal on the house.'

'I will,' I said, accepting with alacrity. 'And bring a bottle of Pouilly Fuissé. It'll go very well with the poached salmon.'

It was a nice way to avert a potentially embarrassing situation, where, in the words of Maggie Smith, one has 'omelette sur le visage'.

Sir Cedric Hardwicke, who really made his name in the Birmingham productions of Shaw's plays, used to claim that the handsomest compliment ever paid to him was by Shaw, who once told him: 'You are my fifth favourite actor, the first four being the Marx Brothers.'

Apart from professional colleagues, audiences can frequently unnerve an actor, too. They do not need to barrack: an overheard comment or whisper can be more disturbing than direct abuse. Hermione Gingold was in the middle of one of her matinée performances in revue when a child's voice broke the silence of the spell-bound audience asking: 'Mummy, what is that lady *for?*'

During a production of *Waiting for Godot* Peter Bull had the humiliation of overhearing a lady in the stalls saying to a friend: 'I do wish the fat one would go.'

Audiences can be disconcerting in other ways. The wonderful Australian prima donna, Dame Nellie Melba, was taking a curtain call at Covent Garden, when, to her delight, it seemed that the loudest cheers were coming from a band of expatriate Australians in the front of the stalls.

'They're shouting "Auntie Nellie, Auntie Nellie",' she said excitedly.

'I rather think, madam,' replied Sir Thomas Beecham, 'that what they are shouting is "Martinelli, Martinelli".'

Her chagrin over the misinterpretation was probably as great as Dame Edith Evans' when, after the booing of *Gentle Jack*, she remarked consolingly, 'Well, at least I heard one *Bravo!*' and I told her, 'No, they were shouting "Go home!".'

Gladys Cooper's sister, Cissie, was equally misled by an audience when she went on stage for the first time, after acting as her sister's dresser for many years. Although she only had a small part, the audience apparently started to hiss almost as soon as she had come on stage. This happened every night and in the end she came into the wings in tears. Gladys Cooper could not understand what was going wrong and she asked the House Manager to see if he could find out what was the matter. So he slipped into the back of the stalls just as her sister was making her entrance and from where he was standing he heard the audience whispering:

'It's Cissie Cooper, Gladys Cooper's sister... It's Cissie Cooper, Gladys Cooper's sister...'

The poet Robert Southey, who was destined in later life to become Poet Laureate, lived a life of rigidly disciplined academic study. His day was organised with minute precision, a fact of which he was immensely proud. Once asked how he spent his time he outlined his routine thus: 'I rise at five throughout the year; from six until eight I read Spanish, then French, for one hour; Portuguese, next, for half an hour – my watch lying on the table; I translate so long; I make extracts so long; and so for the rest,' consequently exhausting himself in the course of the day. Seemingly unimpressed, his listener's only comment was: 'And pray, when dost thou think, friend?'

Even one's friends can be a source of humiliation at times, as the late Charles Burgess Fry found to his cost. Fry was a man of extraordinary capabilities. An Oxford scholar and a triple blue, he became an outstanding sportsman after university. A first division football player and expert tennis player, he also represented Britain at cricket and athletics, and for a time held the world long jump record. Many years later, when he was well into his seventies, he confided to a friend that he was thinking of opening a racing stables and becoming involved with the Turf. 'In what capacity, Charles,' the friend enquired, 'trainer, jockey or horse?'

A former Bishop of Lincoln also found that the hand of friendship is often accompanied by the voice of censure. While experiencing some difficulty in rising from a park bench he was offered assistance by a little girl:
'That's very kind of you, my dear,' he said. 'But are you really strong enough?'
'Oh yes,' the child answered, 'I've often helped my daddy when he was much drunker than you.'

On the other hand the friendly gesture can frequently be misinterpreted with just the same humiliating effect. Lady Astor was once completely nonplussed by an American sailor outside the Palace of Westminster. Seeing the young man staring in bewilderment at the façade of the House of Commons, she said to him:

'Would you like to go in?'

He answered: 'You're the sort of broad my mother told me to avoid.'

There is also the delightful story in much the same vein about the Queen riding in a landau with a visiting African dignitary. They were riding along quite happily when suddenly one of the horses broke wind with appalling ferocity.

'Oh, I'm awfully sorry,' said the Queen.

'That's quite all right, Your Majesty,' replied her companion. 'If you hadn't spoken, I'd have thought it was the horse.'

Of course, humiliation is one way of silencing the boring or foolish, and of ridiculing the self-important. The early nineteenth-century wit and practical joker, Theodore Hook, approached an exceedingly over-dressed man in the Strand to ask him: 'Pray, sir, may I ask if you are anybody in particular?'

An ardent admirer came up to James Joyce in the street one day and asked:

'May I kiss the hand that wrote *Ulysses*?'

'No,' said Joyce. 'It did lots of other things as well.'

At a trial held in Ireland, Sir Edward Carson succeeded in demolishing a prosecution witness with four questions.

'Are you a teetotaller?' he first asked.

'No, I am not.'

'Are you a moderate drinker?'

The witness gave no answer.

'Should I be right if I called you a heavy drinker?'

'That's my business.'

'Have you any other business?' asked Carson triumphantly.

At the end of another case the trial judge questioned Carson privately on the marked difference between two witnesses he had called. One, a carpenter, had been a model witness: clear, succinct and transparently honest. Carson's other witness, by contrast, had been vague, shifty and contradictory; he was a publican. What was the explanation, asked the judge.

'Yet another case of the difference between the bench and the bar,' Carson replied.

The famous Berlin artist, Max Liebermann, who became the leading German impressionist, was a portrait painter of great renown. Infuriated by the incessant chatter of one of his subjects, he silenced her by saying: 'Another word from you, and I paint you as you are.'

Though not pestered by their subjects, great composers are frequently tormented by aspiring musicians. Rossini was once called upon to listen to two pieces composed by a young Italian and then state which of the two he preferred. After playing the first, the young man was reaching for the score of the second, when Rossini stopped him: 'There is no need to play further,' he told him. 'I much prefer the second.'

After auditioning a baritone for a forthcoming production of *Carmen*, Sir Thomas Beecham told the man's agent: 'He's made a mistake. He thinks he's the bull instead of the toreador.'

I have always found that those who make fools of themselves, when they should know better, are seldom tolerated by their peers. A barrister, presenting his case before Lord Clare, felt it necessary to introduce an eagle while pleading on behalf of his client. He then proceeded to apply a complicated metaphor in relation to the bird and eventually became so confused that he completely lost the thread of what he was saying: 'The next time, sir,' commented the Chancellor, 'that you bring an eagle into court, I recommend that you clip its wings.'

Churchill had occasion to rebuke one of his generals during the war for his pompous assumption that 'putting the troops in the picture was the sort of familiarity that breeds contempt'. 'You know, general,' Churchill told him, 'without a certain amount of familiarity, it is extraordinarily difficult to breed anything at all.'

At the turn of the nineteenth century certain London clubs were subjected to periodic police raids, in an attempt to stamp out illicit gambling. On one such occasion police entered the Beefsteak Club and questioned all those present. Asked to identify themselves, three men dining together at a table politely complied. One claimed to be the Belgian envoy, another said he was the Speaker of the House of Commons.

'And I suppose that you are the Prime Minister of England?' enquired one of the officers of the third man.

'Yes, as a matter of fact I am,' answered Lord Balfour.

During a tour of New York, Balfour was shown over one of the city's most recent and tallest skyscrapers. He was told how much it had cost to build, how many men had been employed in its construction, how long it had taken to build and how fast the lifts travelled.

'Dear me, how remarkable,' he murmured. Finally his guide informed him that the building was so solid that it would easily last for a thousand years.

'Dear, dear me, what a great pity.'

In my own opinion bores are the most deserving candidates for the humiliating retort. Beau Brummell received a call one morning from a notoriously dull visitor who treated him to a tediously lengthy account of a recent tour he had made of the north of England. When he finally noticed Brummell's wandering attention, he asked his host which of the lakes he preferred. Turning to his valet, Brummell asked:

'Robinson, which of the lakes do I admire?'

'Windermere, sir.'

'Windermere,' Brummell replied to his visitor. 'So it is, Windermere.'

Prince Philip flew to a local airport to attend a public function in the neighbourhood. When he descended the steps from the plane, he was met by the leader of the reception committee. Thinking of nothing better to say, the wretched man asked what his flight had been like.

'Have you ever flown in a plane?' asked the Duke.

'Oh, yes, your Royal Highness, often.'

'Well, it was just like that.'

When the Israeli statesman, Moshe Dayan, was stopped in his car for speeding, he told the military policeman who had pulled him over, 'I have only one eye. What do you want me to watch – the speedometer or the road?'

Invective

... *he can't be all bad*

Invective

At some time in our lives we have all had cause to inveigh against particular people or things that have made our blood boil for one reason or another. Invective is like steam. Let out in an uncontrolled burst, it disappears harmlessly into the atmosphere. Released in a measured blast and aimed in a specific direction, it scalds.

'Any man who hates little children and small dogs can't be all bad,' said W. C. Fields, incurring the wrath of some people, but the rest of us love it because there are occasions when we all loathe small dogs and crying babies. Actors have always found their competition irksome.

I have had to play with children and animals on countless occasions. Once in a film sequence I had to take a chimpanzee with me in a taxi. We had to take a taxi because the bus-conductor wouldn't allow us on board, but when it drew up alongside, the driver leaned out of the window and said to the chimpanzee: 'I'll take you, but not your mate.'

Catharsis is fine for those who want to purge themselves vicariously of malevolent thoughts and feelings. As Milton puts it at the end of *Samson Agonistes*, crystallising the audience reaction after witnessing the spectacle of great tragedy:

His servants he with new acquist
Of true experience from this great event
With peace and consolation hath dismissed,
And calm of mind all passion spent.

But there are many occasions when there is nothing better than a really well-aimed dig at some pestering moron or arch-rival.

Toler, later Lord Chief Justice, was approached by a craven barrister for a donation of a shilling towards the funeral expenses of an impecunious colleague. 'Only a shilling to bury an attorney?' said Toler. 'Here is a guinea; go and bury one and twenty of them.'

Benjamin Disraeli evidently took great delight in commenting on the Whig leader, Lord John Russell: 'If a traveller were informed that such a man was leader of the House of Commons, he might begin to comprehend how the Egyptians worshipped an insect.'

Russell's successor, W. E. Gladstone, frequently felt the rough edge of Disraeli's tongue and even that of those who were more sympathetic to his cause:

'He has not a single redeeming defect' – *Benjamin Disraeli*.

'Mr Gladstone speaks to me as if I were a public meeting' – *Queen Victoria*.

'I don't object to the Old Man's always having the ace of trumps up his sleeve, but merely to his belief that God Almighty put it there' – *Henry Labouchère (a fellow Whig)*.

However, Gladstone did not suffer fools. He was strongly tempted by a handsome seventeenth-century portrait of a Spanish nobleman and made an offer to buy it. But the dealer refused to lower his price and as Gladstone knew what he was asking was excessive, he left the gallery empty-handed.

When he next saw the painting, it was gracing the drawing-room of a wealthy businessman, with whom he was dining.

'It's a portrait of one of my ancestors,' explained his host, 'at the court of Queen Elizabeth.'

'Three pounds less and he would have been one of my ancestors,' replied Gladstone.

Asquith's daughter, Lady Violet Bonham Carter, had little time for the great Labour politician, Sir Stafford Cripps. Cripps was a genius in the pure sense of the word. His scholarship papers at Oxford were so outstanding that he was persuaded by Sir William Ramsay to work in his laboratory in London instead. He was only twenty-two when his first scientific paper was read before the Royal Society. However, Lady Violet dismissed him airily: 'Sir Stafford has a brilliant mind, until it is made up.'

During his time in the House, Jeremy Thorpe reversed this with his own assessment of a female member of the Labour front bench. 'Mrs Castle,' he stated, 'is an inverted version of Lord Kitchener.'

•••

And talking of Lords, when the formidable figure of Quintin Hogg, arrayed in the Lord Chancellor's full wig and gown, spotted MP Neil Marten behind a group of American tourists in the Palace of Westminster, he cried out, 'Neil!' – and all the tourists did.

•••

The American journalist James Thurber obviously did not share the general opinion of the home-spun philosophy of the ex-Ziegfeld Follies comedian, Will Rogers, which, admirers claimed, nearly moved nations: 'This bosom friend of senators and congressmen,' wrote Thurber, 'was about as daring as an early Shirley Temple.'

French novelist François Mauriac took the wind out of the sails of Jean-Paul Sartre by commenting: 'Sartre's thirst for martyrdom isn't enough to put someone so incurably inoffensive into prison.' And another Gallic wit, Jean Cocteau, told of the man 'who put a chameleon on a tartan rug and watched it die of over-exertion'.

John Dryden, whose own literary career was spent satirising political and professional enemies, was given short shrift by Macaulay, who claimed that: 'His imagination resembles the wings of an ostrich.'

Sir Thomas Beecham reserved his choicest denigrations for those works that he totally abhorred. Elgar's A flat symphony was, he insisted: 'The musical equivalent of St Pancras station.'

Oscar Wilde's well-known censure of the down-to-earth dullard frightens all those who have fallen into the trap of uttering similar platitudes: 'The man who could call a spade a spade should be compelled to use one. It is the only thing he is fit for.'

Bernard Shaw was equally scathing of one of the leading artistic patrons of the late 1890s: 'He's a man of great common sense and good taste ... meaning thereby a man without originality or moral courage.'

Of course Shaw saw himself as having more than just a talent to amuse or satirise. In consequence he never accepted the supremacy of the Bard. In his *Dramatic Opinions* he wrote:

'With the single exception of Homer, there is no eminent writer, not even Sir Walter Scott, whom I can despise so entirely as I despise Shakespeare when I measure my mind against his. It would positively be a relief to dig him up and throw stones at him.'

Although I admire Shaw, I think his castigation here is a little too heavy. Shakespeare's vocabulary alone is a continual source of wonder and delight. Samuel Johnson acknowledged this and, after the Swan of Avon, his must be the most extensive vocabulary in English. Unlike Shaw, he had to come to terms with many physical adversities in life and he faced them stoically. After humiliating years of penury, he combined dignity and self-esteem when writing those marvellous lines refusing Lord Chesterfield's long overdue offer of money:

'The notice which you have been pleased to take of my labours, had it been early, had been kind; but it has been delayed till I am indifferent, and cannot enjoy it; till I am solitary, and cannot impart it; till I am known, and do not want it.'

Johnson suffered from epilepsy and must have known a great deal of intense pain. When he was dying his agony was such that he was found trying to stab himself under the bedclothes. In spite of all this he remained kind and charitable and only came back with a crushing retort and cutting riposte to those whom he felt deserved it. Apart from Chesterfield there was the tedious Oxford don who said to him over dinner one evening:

'Sir, do you not think that life is often boring?'

'Yes,' said Johnson, 'especially if one is sitting next to you.'

Like so many great literary figures Johnson was always in demand as a critic. There was one tiresome woman who was constantly demanding that he read an execrable tragedy that she had written. After putting her off on countless occasions, Johnson was finally forced to refuse once and for all. He told her that if she read it through carefully herself, she would find all the things that he was likely to correct were he to do it.

'But sir,' she persisted, 'I have no time, I have already so many irons in the fire.'

'Why then, madam, the best thing I can advise you to do is to put your tragedy along with your irons.' That was a proper rebuke to someone who in his opinion should have known better.

But Johnson never indulged in cheap contumely. He never attacked those who could not fend for themselves. When his Negro servant was insulted by Mrs Thrale and the servants below stairs and he found that the boy had run off, Johnson took the post-chaise and went galloping after him. He found him crying over his humiliation, but Johnson told him, 'Don't bother about them, Sir. Don't pay any attention to them, Sir,' and embraced him warmly. It is a superb example of sheer affection and abounding evidence of his overriding sense of humanity.

Another facet of his compassion is illustrated by the incident when he and Boswell took a boat from Temple Stairs to Greenwich, which is quite a long way and for which the fare was one penny. On the way Boswell asked the Doctor provocatively if he thought universal education would be a good thing. Johnson stoutly maintained that everyone should have the advantage of an education, and to prove his point he leaned forward to the young boy who was rowing them and asked him: 'Boy, what would you give to know about the Argonauts?' Whereupon the boy leaned upon his oars reflectively and answered: 'Well, Sir, I would give what I have.'

Boswell said it was the one time in their relationship when the Doctor made no reply. But, at Greenwich stairs he saw him give the boy a double tip. For once in his life Johnson didn't bother to reply: he was moved and delighted by the directness and honesty which he admired and adored.

Jibing

Democracy – 'the art of running a circus from the monkey cage'

The timely sneer or jibe is an unbeatable means of maliciously deflating or dismissing objects of contempt. I remember an occasion when the producer, John Perry, was having a running battle with the agent of one of the stars in Sandy Wilson's *The Buccaneer* which he was presenting and in which I played. The star in question was Betty Warren and she had been promised bottom billing with her name appearing in large type with an 'and' in front of it. However, it kept appearing without the 'and', so the agent kept ringing John Perry to complain. Finally, when the agent remonstrated:

'Where's her "and", there's no "and". It should be "and Betty Warren". She's very angry about this, it should have an "and",' John Perry cried out:

'If she's not very careful it will be "but",' and slammed down the receiver.

Florenz Ziegfeld once offered Gracie Allen $750 a week to appear in one of his London shows. That sounded good to her, but she asked Ziegfeld what the fee would be if George Burns, her husband and straight man, appeared with her.

'Five hundred' was the answer.

The important thing about the good jibe is that it should contain an element of truth, albeit slightly embellished. Sir Seymour Hicks epitomised this in his comment on marriage: 'A man does not buy his wife a fur coat to keep her warm, but to keep her pleasant.'

Nancy Banks-Smith had this to say on contemporary design: 'In my experience, if you have to keep the lavatory door shut by extending your left leg, it's modern architecture.'

H. L. Mencken, who always had a rather jaundiced view of orthodox institutions, used to describe democracy as: 'The art of running a circus from the monkey cage.'

H. G. Wells did not hold the Catholic faith in very high esteem. He used to summarise its edicts as: 'Confessions on Saturday. Absolution on Sunday. At it again on Monday.'

The eighteenth-century wit and cleric Sydney Smith had little regard for the Prince Regent and even less for his excessively extravagant lifestyle. Visiting Brighton for the first time after the completion of the Royal Pavilion, Smith remarked scornfully: 'It is as though St Paul's had gone down to the sea and pupped.'

The Prince's uncle, the Duke of Gloucester, showed delightful, but no doubt completely innocent, irreverence for the great Edward Gibbon, at the time when he was the foremost scholar in the land. When the first volume of his mammoth *Decline and Fall of the Roman Empire* was published, the Duke showed an interest in the work and Gibbon duly presented him with a copy. Later on, he went to give His Royal Highness the second volume. The Duke received him warmly and without even opening the book laid it on the table saying: 'Another damn'd thick, square book! Always scribble, scribble, scribble, eh! Mr Gibbon.'

Characteristically, Groucho Marx was less affable when he met the author of a recently published novel: 'From the moment I picked up your book until I put it down, I was convulsed with laughter,' he told the delighted author, adding, 'Some day, I intend to read it.'

The American detective-story writer Rex Stout bought a plot of land on top of a hill in Danbury, Connecticut, where he built a fourteen-room house with his own hands. When it was finished he invited Frank Lloyd Wright to pay a visit and give his opinion. The celebrated architect duly arrived, took some time looking around and then commented:

'A superb spot. Someone should build a house here.'

One of my favourite stories about Johnson is the occasion at a reception given in his honour in 1755, the year of the publication of his great dictionary. It is another perfect example of his total directness. In the course of the reception a lady came up to him and congratulated him for excluding any rude or vulgar words from his work. 'And just how do you know that there are none there, madam, unless you were looking for them?' he enquired. The prude got no change from the lexicographer.

Although the fourth Earl of Chesterfield drew that indignant letter from Johnson after his years of neglect, he achieved fame for his own wit. This is preserved for posterity in the *Letters to his Son*, written to imbue the boy with the manners and standards of a man of the world. Johnson, admittedly, dismissed the whole of this *oeuvre*: 'They inculcate the morals of a whore and the manners of a dancing master.' Nevertheless, they contain a series of witty, elegant, cynical and exquisitely phrased observations on contemporary society and mores. Chesterfield was evidently as sharp in his conversation, as the exchange with Elizabeth Chudleigh, Countess of Bristol and self-styled Duchess of Kingston, shows. The Countess was widely rumoured to have given birth to illegitimate twins.

'My Lord,' she said to Chesterfield, 'I hope that you do not believe these abominable rumours about me which are circulating everywhere.'

'You have no need to be distressed, madam,' he replied. 'I very rarely believe more than half of what I hear.'

Bernard Shaw has become legendary for the persistent jibes he made against the follies of his society and the fools who perpetuated them. During the course of conversation at dinner one evening he asked one esteemed lady seated next to him if she would go to bed with a man for five hundred pounds. The lady replied mischievously:

'Well, it would depend on how good looking he was.'

'Would you do it for ten bob, then?' asked Shaw.

'What do you take me for?' exclaimed the lady indignantly.

'We have already settled that,' said Shaw drily. 'All we are doing now is agreeing the price.'

As an American, James Whistler had the advantage in England of being able to strike a discordant note, whenever he wished, which he did with unnerving regularity. During the Boer War he was a guest at a dinner-table at which the conversation was dominated by the recent action of the British commander, Sir Redvers Buller. Buller, the other guests claimed, had retreated across the Modder river without losing a man, a flag, or a gun. 'Or a minute,' added Whistler.

Shaw once received an invitation from a society hostess, whose company he could not abide. Replying to the invitation, which stated that she would be 'at home' at a specified hour on a certain date, Shaw replied: 'G. B. S. also.'

Children's parties demand a sense of resolve and vigour all of their own. Such a gathering was held at the Palace of Westminster one Christmas, to entertain the off-spring of members of Parliament and members of the palace staff. Among the grown-ups supervising the proceedings was Margaret Thatcher, who moved briskly between the tables helping to dish out tea. One small boy, who took exception to what had been placed in front of him, complained:

'Miss ... miss! You've given me blancmange and I don't like blancmange.'

'That,' she answered, 'is what parties are all about: eating food you don't like.'

I dislike parties myself and generally throw the invitations into the waste-paper bin, but one that I didn't discard came from Downing Street, inviting me to a dinner which Harold Wilson was giving for the Swedish Prime Minister. In exquisite copper-plate, it requested me to reply to the Private Secretary, so I wrote back: 'Thank you for the invite, but lack-a-day and rue I haven't the clothes for these grand occasions. Alas, I find them all too inhibiting. Sincerely yours...' I kept the card though, a huge pasteboard affair with gold round the edges, which made a very good bookmark.

Beau Brummell must have been quite the reverse. As a leader of fashion in Regency society a word of reproof from him was tantamount to social approbation. On being told of a young buck who was so well dressed that he had turned everyone's heads, he commented: 'In that case he was not well dressed.'

'I hold the umbrella over my head'

Knock-out

Probably the most satisfying acid drops are those that leave the listener absolutely speechless, and perhaps the most pleasing are the completely unintentional knock-outs, which though innocently delivered have the startling effect of bringing any conversation to an abrupt halt. Children are often excellent value when it comes to these.

•••

Maggie Smith told me how she was forever telling one of her children, Christopher, to eat his food properly, because he was always picking at it and leaving most of it on the plate. One day she said in desperation:

'Eat that food, Christopher! It's very, very good.'

To which he replied: 'What's it supposed to be?'

'It's a potato in its jacket.'

'I don't care if it's in its trousers, I'm not eating it,' he answered.

•••

The juxtaposition of total innocence with total annihilation is always hilarious to those not on the receiving end. Mrs Einstein scored a notable triumph in America when she visited the Mt Wilson Observatory in California. She was shown over the giant telescope and given a detailed explanation of its operation by the principal astronomer. Laboriously he explained: 'One of the principal functions of all this sophisticated paraphernalia is to find out the shape of the Universe.'

'Oh, my husband does that,' she said, 'on the back of an old envelope.'

In the course of a train journey to New York, the mother of Carson McCullers, the American novelist and playwright, got into conversation with a pleasant lady of aristocratic *mien* with whom she was sharing her compartment. Noticing that her companion appeared to be fond of reading, Mrs McCullers' mother said that she was going to visit her daughter, who was a writer, and then embarked on a detailed description of her various literary accomplishments. The other lady listened with interest and then mentioned that her father had also been a writer. What was his name, Mrs McCullers' mother asked.

'Count Tolstoy' was the answer.

Most knock-outs are delivered with all the premeditated force and skill of a winning punch. They are the *coups de grâce* which silence unfortunate victims once and for all. Before his downfall in 1964, Nikita Khrushchev was addressing a large audience in the Soviet Union, at which he was denouncing the evils of Stalin. In the middle of his speech a voice rang out from the back of the hall, asking:

'Why didn't you restrain Stalin? You were one of his colleagues, after all.'

A deathly hush fell on the assembly. No one moved. Khrushchev ran his eyes across the rows of seats and thundered:

'Who said that?'

Still no one moved. The tension became unbearable, until Khrushchev quietly said:

'Now you know why.'

Noël Coward was never one to suffer foolishness or impertinence lightly, and since an awful lot of actors are dreadful egomaniacs, he became very accomplished at delivering stunning ripostes. There are always one or two members of a cast who are rather self-indulgent. They go on and on about their own theory of acting, regardless of the boredom inflicted on the rest of the company. Coward had one of these in a production of his and the man rambled on about motivation and meaning in his character until Coward became utterly exasperated. He told him: 'Your motivation is your pay packet at the end of the week. Now get on with it.'

The self-important and pushy were dismissed with similarly devastating rejoinders. An eager admirer pushed through a crowd gathered around Coward as he was leaving a hotel in New York after a brief visit:

'You remember me?' said the woman. 'I met you with Douglas Fairbanks.'

'Madam,' replied Coward, 'I don't even remember Douglas Fairbanks.'

The devastating, blunt rejoinder has often been delivered by leading theatrical figures to the fawning and the sycophantic. Lionel Barrymore was interviewed by a young reporter about his career, when he was well into his declining years. Asked by the young man if acting was as much fun as it used to be, Barrymore answered him: 'Young man, I am seventy-five. Nothing is as much fun as it used to be.'

Sir Cedric Hardwicke was asked by an interviewer how he chose his parts, to which he replied: 'I read the contract first.'

Sir Herbert Beerbohm Tree must have given little comfort to the melancholy friend who came to consult him on whether he should drown his sorrows in drink, or commit suicide. 'Is life really worth living?' he asked Tree, only to receive the reply: 'That depends on the liver.'

Tree was showing Sir Squire Bancroft round his new theatre, His Majesty's, with unashamed pride. After the extensive tour he asked his fellow actor-manager what he thought of it. 'A great many windows to clean' was Bancroft's impassive reply.

Many actors have to wear ridiculous costumes at some time in their careers, but few have carried off the embarrassment as stylishly as Mrs Patrick Campbell when she played the blind Egyptian in the 1909 production of *False Gods*. The wardrobe department had swathed her in a tight-fitting costume of gaudy black and yellow in which she hobbled about the stage in a manner befitting her visual handicap. As she shuffled into the wings one evening she was met by Graham Robertson, who told her in awed terms that she looked magnificent. 'Nonsense,' she told him. 'I look like an elderly wasp in an interesting condition,' and hobbled off to her dressing room.

I was in a revue once that had a sketch that ran along similar lines; it was the first stand-up comedy that I had done in revue. I used to come on with a hollow tree-stump that I put down in the middle of the stage. 'The birds all know me,' I confided to the audience, sticking twigs into my hair and explaining that I was disguising myself as a tree in order to study the tits at close quarters. There followed a long dissertation on the gullibility of our feathered friends, *à la* Ludwig Koch, with cracks like 'in winter we see the Blue Tits', and finally I told the audience, 'If it comes on to rain I unfurl my large umbrella and hold it over my head, thus. People say to me, "But doesn't that ruin the camouflage? Surely when the birds see your umbrella, they will know you are not a tree." To which I reply: "Maybe, but I'm not getting wet for a load of bleeding birds."'

One of the most amusing stage 'knock-outs' I know is the one recounted by Ben Travers which was delivered to him by Charles Hawtrey. The great man had been engaged to direct Travers' first farce *The Dippers* and the nervous young playwright had been summoned to attend the first rehearsal. To his horror he arrived to find Hawtrey systematically working his way through the best scene in the play with a red pencil, cutting great chunks out of the dialogue. Travers stood there timidly watching as his brain-child was gradually whittled away. Finally the pencil point came to his favourite line in the play, halted momentarily, and then struck through it.

'Oh, Mr Hawtrey,' exclaimed Travers, 'that last line. Must that go? I'm sorry, but really I always thought that was rather a good line.'

'A good line?' repeated Hawtrey slowly, 'a good line? It's a very good line indeed, dear boy. You mustn't on any account lose it. Put it in another play.'

• • •

Archbishop Frederick Temple used to tell a story of much the same hurt pride. Ever since his days at Blundells he had enjoyed community singing, and, often turning his collar round, he never missed the chance to join in a rousing hymn or carol during his five years as Archbishop of Canterbury. On one of his visits around the country he was passing a church when the sound of lusty singing lured him inside. Squeezing into a space in a pew he picked up a hymn book and joined in. After he had sung no more than a couple of verses, the man standing next to him nudged him in the side and said under his breath: 'Dry up, mister. You're spoiling the show.'

• • •

Failure to recognise people has led many public figures to receive tart replies on numerous occasions. Sir Thomas Beecham was returning to his hotel after conducting the Hallé Orchestra in a concert in Manchester, when he noticed a distinguished-looking lady chatting with a group of people near the lift in the foyer. Knowing that he could not slip past without catching her attention, but realising, too, that he had forgotten her name, Beecham paused to speak with her for a moment before pressing for the lift. He was about to conclude their brief exchange of pleasantries when he suddenly remembered that she had a brother, and with the hope of identifying her, he asked how her brother was and if he was still in the same job. 'Oh, he is very well,' she replied, 'and he is still King.'

Knock-outs have been achieved in other ways as well. Hollywood sex-goddesses have frequently lived up to being blonde bombshells in words as well as looks. Mae West remarked to a pugilist after hearing a lengthy explanation of his art: 'Honey, if it's all-in, why wrestle?'

Marilyn Monroe was asked by an interviewer: 'Isn't it true you once posed for photographs with nothing on?' and answered him: 'Oh no, I had the radio on.'

Closer to home is the story Lady Veronica McLeod, only daughter of a general stationed in India and one of the foremost beauties of London society in the 1890s. At the age of nineteen she sailed to India to spend a few months with her parents. Every man aboard fell in love with her, but she reserved her favours for a handsome steward in second-class. After dancing together at the ship's fancy-dress ball, they ended the night in her ladyship's bedroom. Her beau was up and serving breakfast long before Lady Veronica awoke. When he caught up with her later in the day, she returned his familiarity with chill disdain. 'In the circles in which I move,' she reminded him, 'sleeping with a woman does not constitute an introduction.'

The harsh realities of life, stringently commented upon, can have just as deflating an effect. Sir Walter Scott was taking a stroll around Abbotsford with his wife one spring morning, when they came across a field of ewes good-naturedly suffering the high jinks of their playful offspring.

'Ah,' mused Scott, ''tis no wonder that poets from ages past have made the lamb the emblem of peace and innocence.'

'They are indeed delightful animals,' agreed Lady Scott, 'especially with mint sauce.'

Lord Rothschild sent a cabman away with a flea in his ear after the man had complained that the tip he had just been given was only half that received from Rothschild's son a few days earlier. 'I know,' said his lordship. 'My son has a millionaire for a father. I haven't.'

Lord Rutherford, one of the great pioneers of nuclear physics, was a man not unduly self-conscious about his worldly success.

'You're always on the crest of a wave, my lord,' one deferential interviewer told him.

'I know,' said Rutherford, 'but after all, I made the wave, didn't I?'

Sir Arthur Wellesley, the first Duke of Wellington, had a characteristically brusque way of dealing with sycophants. One poor wretch who said to the Duke on being presented to him:

'This is the proudest moment of my life, my lord', was told:

'Don't be a fool, sir.'

A member who had recently joined the Garrick Club made the mistake with Sir Henry Irving. Keen to claim Irving as an acquaintance, he greeted him cheerily, 'Hello, Irving. An extraordinary thing has just happened to me. A total stranger stopped me in the street and said, "God bless me, is that you?"'

'And... er... was it?' asked Irving.

On the other hand Samuel Wilberforce, a nineteenth-century Bishop of Oxford who was nicknamed 'Soapy Sam' for his ability to talk his way out of almost any situation, was thrown into a quandary when asked to admire a particularly ugly baby. Staring at the child for some seconds in apparent amazement, he finally managed: 'Well, that is a baby.'

This was a very commendable effort, especially when the emphasis is laid on the third word of the quotation; if it is read thus, Wilberforce can be seen to have acquitted himself adroitly. By stressing a certain word in a trite phrase, it is possible to wriggle out of all sorts of dilemmas. A friend of mine uses 'What about that?' as a critical exclamation which can be said admiringly or insultingly by altering the accentuation, while he awaits the verdict of his betters. He maintains it's a valuable ploy, which ensures safety where judgements are uncertain and where diplomacy demands complaisance. Most of the time, people accept what they expect to hear and in the unlikely event of a challenge, the form can be redesigned to suit the occasion. When an actor I know was offered a tatty tour, and the agent told him one of the theatres was 'fringe and off-beat', he muttered, 'in a dirty back street'. The agent asked sharply 'What's that?' and he swiftly replied, 'I said that'll be a treat.' This is the *sotto voce* acid drop, which can be recounted with relish.

Lampoon

Cryptic messages of Palaeolithic cynicism

Since time immemorial men have been making scurrilously witty remarks about other individuals. No doubt the work of prehistoric craftsmen, preserved on cave walls around the world, contains cryptic messages of Palaeolithic cynicism, as yet undeciphered. The Roman poet, Catullus, writing in the first century BC, offered this two-line lampoon to the world's greatest leader:

'Complete indifference to your welfare, Caesar,
is matched only by ignorance of who you are.'

From then on lampoons have flourished in published works and private discourse. Stylish, humorous and malicious, they have delighted readers and listeners alike, for, whatever motivated their utterance, they share one factor in common – they were all intended for public consumption.

The Revd Sydney Smith used to take some personal credit for the discovery of Macaulay's genius when he was still young and unknown. However, Smith shared with many others certain misgivings about his protégé. 'There are no limits to his knowledge, on small subjects as well as great,' he told one listener. 'He is like a book in breeches.' Asked about recent changes in Macaulay's conversation which had always been excessively domineering, Smith answered: '...he has occasional flashes of silence that make his conversation perfectly delightful.'

The nineteenth-century American politician, Thaddeus Stevens, was asked by Abraham Lincoln whether his fellow politician, Simon Cameron, was an honest man.

'He would not steal a red-hot stove,' Stevens replied.

Sometime later he was taken to task over this slur on his colleague's name, which he finally recanted:

'I said Cameron would not steal a red-hot stove. I now withdraw that statement.'

Calvin Coolidge, the twenty-ninth President of the United States, was a man noted for his taciturnity. H. L. Mencken held him in no great esteem as a politician and commented on his years in office: 'Nero fiddled, but Coolidge only snored.'

If Coolidge is famous for things he did not say, Churchill is undeniably famous for the things he did say in his many stirring speeches. The influence of the Bible is evident in his use of the triple-stress which he employed with superb effect. The King James version has an elegant simplicity, eschewing the polysyllabic to produce matchless lines like: 'Suffer the little children to come unto me, and forbid them not: for of such is the kingdom of Heaven'. The New Testament warns us against the excessive and against obsessive piety and records that Jesus didn't despise the company of harlots and publicans. Churchill, too, disliked any kind of pretension and in a murmured aside apropos Stafford Cripps, a politician of great austerity, unmatched piety and rigid teetotalism, he said: 'There, but for the grace of God, goes God.'

The great lampooners have been writers and poets for the most part. Surely the greatest in the last hundred years has been Oscar Wilde, who, taking up the pen of former masters like Dryden, Pope, Swift and Sheridan, has left us with many memorable satires on his peers, of which these are a handful of my favourites:

While staying with Frank Harris in a hotel in New York, he wrote to a friend: 'Frank Harris is upstairs, thinking about Shakespeare at the top of his voice.'

And of Shaw, he said: 'Bernard Shaw is an excellent man; he has not an enemy in the world, but he is thoroughly disliked by his friends.'

During his viva voce examination in Divinity, at Oxford, Wilde was asked to translate orally a passage from the Greek version of the New Testament. Presented with the account of Christ's Passion, Wilde proceeded to translate quickly and fluently to the evident satisfaction of the examiners. After he had worked his way through a number of verses the Chairman of the examiners told him that he could stop. However, he ignored this and continued with his translation. After a second request they succeeded in stopping him, but only so that he could say: 'Oh, do let me go on. I want to see how it finishes.'

• • •

Wilde's lampoons did not stop there:

'Henry James writes fiction as if it were a painful duty.' (William Faulkner took an equally dim view of this novelist, saying on one occasion that: 'Henry James is one of the nicest old ladies I've ever met.')

'George Moore wrote brilliant English until he discovered grammar.'

'The gods have bestowed on Max [Beerbohm] the gift of perpetual old age.'

'He has one of those characteristic British faces that, once seen, are never remembered.'

• • •

Whistler complemented this last observation with his maxim on the English woman: 'She succeeds, as no other can, in obliging men to forget her sex.'

Noël Coward warned a friend about a mutual acquaintance with this guarded advice: 'He's a little man, that's his trouble. Never trust a man with short legs... brains too near their bottoms.'

Stephen Spender used to describe W. H. Auden's face as: 'A wedding cake left out in the rain.'

Asked if he knew what an extravaganza was, Groucho Marx answered: 'I ought to know. I married one.'

Margot Asquith once remarked of her husband, the Liberal Prime Minister: 'His modesty amounts to deformity.'

When Ramsay MacDonald became Prime Minister, Churchill remarked: 'We know that he has, more than any other man, the gift of compressing the largest amount of words into the smallest amount of thought.'

The novelist Arnold Bennett described the prominent social reformers Sydney and Beatrice Webb as: 'Two of the nicest people if ever there was one.'

During the court action taken by Sir James Goldsmith against the magazine *Private Eye*, the editor, Richard Ingrams, failed to obey an injunction and ran a strong risk of being put in prison. Looking on his pending fate philosophically, he mused: 'The only thing I really worry about in going to prison is the thought of Lord Longford coming to visit me.'

Salvador Dali used to take his pet ocelot with him when he was out and about. Once, in New York, he tied the animal's lead to the leg of a table while he stopped for a cup of coffee in a restaurant. A woman passing by, on her way to the door, spotted Dali's pet and exclaimed in alarm, 'What on earth is that?'

'It's only a cat,' Dali reassured her, 'I've painted it over with an op-art design.'

Relieved, but now embarrassed by her reaction, the woman took a closer look and told Dali, 'Now I can see what it is. At first I thought it was a real ocelot.'

Malice

'How can they tell?'

Malice is often an essential part of humour and conversely humour is often a primary ingredient in malice. One can't deny there are some individuals whose behaviour merits nothing short of malice pure and simple. There always will be tiresome people unwilling to accept their limitations; they aspire to a role they can't properly play. I have met those who feel they must try to be funny with a comedian. I once came across an hotel manager who was a case in point. Asking him to clear a cluttered room, I said:

'Would you remove the stool from the bathroom? I'm not in my dotage, I can have a bath, without the aid of a stool. And will you please remove the television, I don't want to watch that rubbish. And will you please remove that large bin marked Sanitary Towels.'

'Oh, don't you use them?' he smiled.

'I'm full of tricks, dear,' I replied, 'but that doesn't happen to be one of them.'

Some actors have to be treated equally harshly. They become so wrapped up in themselves that, apart from being dreadful bores, they are impossible to work with. The essential element in boredom is self-absorption.

People who totally lack self-awareness are always the most tedious; the unselfish are those who are aware of the need for reciprocity. I have mentioned earlier Noël Coward's exemplary treatment of such nuisances, and Hitchcock's forthright remark that: 'Actors should be treated like cattle.' Over-involvement with method acting, motivation and interpretation is self-centred. It is more concerned with conceit than with the ensemble effect of a production. Self-absorption once led an actor to stare endlessly at the stage cloth and caused director Jack Minster to protest: 'Don't look at the floor, boy. You won't find anything down there... except the bloody play.'

Tyrone Guthrie was another director with a unique ability to cut through pretension. 'Never mind interpretation, choreography, costumes and lighting,' he said, 'the director's first duty is to create an atmosphere in which the artist becomes uninhibited.' When he was directing the Bishops in *Henry VIII*, he said, 'Lot of black tea cosies, rush across the stage, look for the King, see he's not there, pee your drawers, run back, have another look, yes he's coming, compose yourselves, everything's all right.' As a mise-en-scène for the entrance of the King it was masterly.

When the boot has been on the other foot, however, self-indulgent directors have been put in their places in no uncertain terms. During one of her many stage appearances in New York, Ellen Terry was engaged at great expense to play Portia, one of the roles in which she excelled. To direct her the management had brought in a bright young American director, bristling with new ideas. Every scene was choreographed with infinite precision. Every gesture and movement was studied with minute care and had to be executed with equal accuracy. After suffering his methods for some time in silence, Miss Terry finally gave voice to her wrath. Guiding her as usual through the text, which she could recite in her sleep, he demonstrated the gestures she was to perform in enticing Bassanio to close the lead casket. After showing her how to turn her head coyly, lift her hand to her cheek and then turn away diffidently, the director was about to run through the scene, when Miss Terry walked up to him and asked: 'When do you want me to do that little something for which you are paying me all this money?'

Although Bernard Shaw had great admiration for the Hungarian director, Gabriel Pascal, there were times when members of his company must have shared Ellen Terry's doubts and frustrations with his methods. Shaw's esteem for Pascal was such that he entrusted him with the filming of several of his plays, *Pygmalion*, *Major Barbara* and the celebrated production of *Caesar and Cleopatra*. It was during the filming of the latter that he gave Claude Rains, who was playing Caesar, several directions which the actor thought quite wrong. An exasperated Rains, dressed in his purple robes and laurel crown, rose from his throne, descended the steps to where Gabriel Pascal was standing behind the camera, and said to him: 'If you're not very careful, I'll play this scene as you want it.'

A young director meeting Athene Seyler, who happened to be his leading lady, for the first time, asked her blankly, 'What have you done?'

Athene, who by that time had been on the stage for over fifty years, answered equally uncomprehendingly:

'Do you mean this morning?'

Presumptuous upstarts have often provoked some fine malicious flourishes. The eighteenth-century Whig, John Wilkes, also after suffering some conceited young oaf's ceaseless exposition of his own virtues at the dinner table, gained his revenge over the port.

'I was born between twelve and one on the first of January,' the young man confided to him. 'Isn't it strange?'

'Not in the slightest,' answered Wilkes. 'You could only have been conceived on the first of April.'

Wilkes' younger contemporary, Richard Porson – whose own literary predilections lay in the ancient world – had little time for the poetry of the early nineteenth century. Shortly before Porson's death in 1808, a friend reported to him this complaint of the poet Robert Southey:

'My "Madoc" has brought me in a mere trifle; but that poem will be a valuable possession to my family.'

'"Madoc" will be read,' Porson informed the mutual acquaintance, 'when Homer and Virgil are forgotten.'

The early nineteenth-century humorist and playwright, Douglas Jerrold, always took a great interest in the work of his friends, especially those who were writers, like himself. Preferring the doctrine of speaking the truth to that of telling white lies, he made it generally known whenever he was disappointed in a friend's latest book.

'I hear you said this was the worst book I ever wrote,' complained one indignant colleague, brandishing his latest publication.

'No, I didn't,' said Jerrold. 'I said that it was the worst book anybody ever wrote.'

Running battles between rivals have always been liberally seasoned with generous measures of malevolence. When Calvin Coolidge died in 1933, and Dorothy Parker was told that the ex-President was dead, she said: 'How can they tell?'

During his years as leader of the Opposition Harold Wilson once remarked of the government front bench: 'Every time Mr Macmillan comes back from abroad, Mr Butler goes to the airport and grips him warmly by the throat.'

An even more ignominious tale circulated during the years of the post-war Labour government, when it was said of its leader: 'An empty taxi drew up at the House of Commons, and Mr Attlee stepped out.'

When Harold Wilson was Prime Minister, he encouraged the belief that as a child he had to go to school without wearing boots. Hearing this, Harold Macmillan commented that if there was any truth in the story, it was probably because Wilson's boots were too small for him.

There was always rather a tense relationship between Sir Herbert Beerbohm Tree and Mrs Patrick Campbell, as there often is between two abrasive figures who have reached the height of the same profession. Tree openly acknowledged his hostility, while Mrs Patrick Campbell could hardly disguise her own outbursts:

'I don't like her,' admitted Tree. 'But don't misunderstand me, my dislike is purely platonic.'

If ever there was a past-master of malice, though, it was W. C. Fields. After his famous pronouncement on small dogs and children he was asked how he really liked children: 'Boiled or fried?' he asked.

Nemesis

'You can stand on your head if you like'

Nemesis

In the ancient pantheon, Nemesis is the goddess of retribution, on whom we rely for sharp, acrid retorts whenever we are insulted, challenged or simply provoked.

One man comes to my mind who must have earnestly invoked this goddess in vain. He was starting an after-dinner speech at the Savoy and rose to test the microphone, asking, 'Can everybody hear me?' A weary voice from the far end of the table replied, 'I can hear you perfectly, but I am willing to change with anyone who can't.' Oh Nemesis, where were you in that hapless speaker's moment of need? Probably away helping others judging from the tone of some of the well-known ripostes of history.

Samuel Johnson was attending a dinner given by a close friend and among the guests was a young man who fancied himself as a wit. Since Johnson was somewhat advanced in years, the youth decided to try his luck at taunting the venerable doctor.

'Tell me this, Sir,' said the young man, 'what would you give to be as young and sprightly as I am?'

'Why, Sir,' said Johnson, 'I should almost be content to be as foolish and conceited.'

At the close of a successful season at the Old Vic, the young John Gielgud, anxious to be taken seriously by his elders in the theatre, explained to Lillian Baylis that much as he wanted to work with her again, he could not begin immediately because he had so many other engagements.

'That's right,' she told him, 'you play all the young parts you can – while you're still able to.'

After Churchill suffered his second stroke, he returned to the Commons tottering painfully into the chamber on a couple of walking sticks. 'The old man's very ga-ga,' one young Tory MP told a friend seated beside him.

'He's also very hard of hearing,' growled Churchill as he shuffled past.

Among John Wilkes' many colourful exploits, which included being expelled from the House of Commons, libelling George III and being outlawed, there was a violent quarrel that he had with Lord Sandwich for many years. When they came face to face by chance in a London club, Sandwich addressed Wilkes:

'Sir, you will either die of the pox or on the gallows.'

To which Wilkes replied: 'That, my lord, depends on whether I embrace your mistress or your principles.'

Winston Churchill, who seems to have collected more than his fair share of female antagonism, was set upon by a fellow guest at dinner one evening, shortly after he had grown himself whiskers.

'Mr Churchill,' the lady said, 'I care neither for your politics nor your moustache.'

'Do not distress yourself,' he told her, 'you are very unlikely to come into contact with either.'

The quarrel between George III's son, the Prince of Wales, and Beau Brummell was even more celebrated than that between John Wilkes and Lord Sandwich. This first came to public attention at a reception that Brummell was giving with his friend, Alvaney. On the announcement of the Prince's arrival, the hosts and two other gentlemen took up positions by the door, holding lighted candles, in order to receive the royal guest. When he arrived the Prince spoke very civilly to the two men standing on his right and then turned to the man next to Brummell, to whom he also paid a polite greeting. When he turned to Brummell, however, he looked right through him, and without so much as a glimmer of recognition walked past into the room.

Just as the Prince was about to greet the other guests, Brummell asked his companion in a loud voice: 'Alvaney, who's your fat friend?' – an aside which cost him his place at court, and in society.

• • •

Lord Byron would probably not have cared about either. For all his faults he could never be accused of being a snob. He was reprimanded by the university authorities on one occasion, because of his friendship with the prize-fighter and champion of all England, John Jackson. In answer to this wholly unjustified remonstration, he told his censors that Gentleman Jackson's manners were: ' ...infinitely superior to those of the fellows of the college whom I met at high table.'

• • •

Benjamin Disraeli was frequently accused of cultivating the opposite type of friendship, which many critics viewed as blatant flattery. Making no attempt to deny their claims, Disraeli confounded them by openly admitting to it: 'You have heard me accused of being a flatterer,' he told Matthew Arnold. 'It is true. I am a flatterer. I have found it useful. Everyone likes flattery; and when it comes to royalty you should lay it on with a trowel.'

Disraeli had other critics who used to accuse him of being a Tory in disguise. These he silenced once and for all by telling them tartly that: 'The closest thing to a Tory in disguise is a Whig in power.'

F. E. Smith was never one of those craven barristers who meekly accepted a judge's rebukes. One leading member of the Queen's Bench told him: 'You are very offensive, young man.' To which he replied:

'As a matter of fact, we both are, and the only difference between us is that I am trying to be, and you can't help it.'

Whistler, like Churchill, occasionally had trouble with women, although he usually had the upper hand. The one notable exception was Lady Meux, who after suffering one of the artist's frequent insults hit back saying: 'You keep a civil tongue in that head of yours, Jimmy, or I'll have in someone to finish those portraits of me.'

Shortly after John Tooke had published two pairs of portraits of fathers and sons (the Pitts and the Foxes), he met Sheridan, whose opinion of his talent was similar in tone to that of Whistler's subject.

'So, sir!' said Sheridan. 'You are the reverend gentleman, I am told, who sometimes amuses himself in drawing portraits.'

'Yes, sir. I am that gentleman,' replied Tooke, 'and if you will do me the favour of sitting for me for yours, I will take it so faithfully, that even you yourself shall shudder at it.'

A century after Sheridan's wit ruled the stage, there were several contenders striving for that coveted position, among them Wilde and W.S. Gilbert.

'I wish I could talk like you,' Gilbert told Wilde one evening, continuing after a momentary pause: 'I'd keep my mouth shut and claim it as a virtue.'

'Ah, that would be selfish,' replied Wilde. 'I could deny myself the pleasure of talking, but not to others the pleasure of listening.'

Gilbert was rehearsing a production of *The Ne'er-do-Well* with Johnston Forbes-Robertson when Forbes-Robertson asked him, as both director and author:

'May I deliver that speech standing instead of sitting?'

'Oh, you can stand on your head, if you like,' Gilbert told him.

'No, I leave that to you.'

Noël Coward employed similar tactics with the late Gilbert Harding who, attending one of Coward's plays in the West End, had fallen asleep quite early in the first act and had continued snoring loudly throughout the rest of the play, in spite of attempts to wake him up. After the show was over he met Coward in the foyer and apologised profusely for his behaviour. 'My dear fellow, there's absolutely no need at all for you to apologise,' Coward told him airily. 'After all, I have never bored you half as much as you have bored me.'

Earlier in his career Coward had repeatedly reproved an actress playing opposite him, because she persisted in dragging out her lines unnecessarily, ruining the whole pace of the scene. Finally, she tired of his reprimands, lost her temper and yelled at him:

'If you go on like that I'll throw something at you.'

To which Coward replied: 'You might start with my cues.'

Lady Diana Cooper was appearing in a profoundly religious play called *The Miracle*, at the same time that Coward was presenting one of his comedies in New York. When they met sometime later she said to him:

'I saw your play, Noël, but I didn't laugh once I'm afraid.'

'Didn't you, darling?' answered Coward. 'I saw yours and simply roared.'

The American writer and actress, Ilka Chase, was divorced from her actor-husband Louis Calhern, when he left her to marry Julia Hoyt. A short time after their final split, Ms Chase was moving house and came across some visiting cards she had ordered in the name of Mrs Louis Calhern. These she promptly posted to her successor with the note:

'Dear Julia, I hope these reach you in time.'

Obloquy

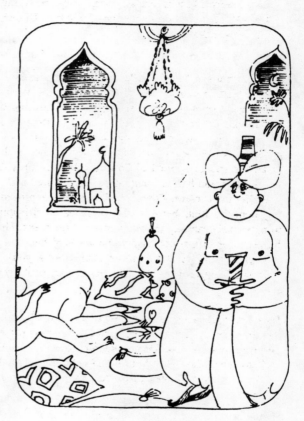

Critics – 'like eunuchs in a harem'

Obloquy

It was once suggested that Shaw should receive some reward for his services in the forthcoming Honours List. The normal discreet enquiries were made to see whether he was in agreement with the proposal. As it transpired, he was not, and he replied to the enquiry that being Bernard Shaw was sufficient honour for any man. I can understand his refusal: once you accept an accolade, you must perforce consider yourself part of the Establishment. Shaw rightly thought, 'No thank you. If I want to satirise you and all your rituals, I must be free to do so.' He knew the obligations implicit in the acceptance of honours. He knew that using humour would inevitably lead him to include satire and obloquy, which would have the specific purpose of taking and exposing in society what he felt to be bogus and meretricious. For this reason he strongly disapproved of the plan by the theatre management of London to club together to give a very rich present to the Lord Chancellor's reader of plays. Admonishing them, he said: 'In my day when a builder gave money to the local council to procure a tender, he did it by stealth and blushed to find it fame.'

Most of us use obloquy for less laudable ends than Shaw; we seldom compose homilies on social mores, preferring instead to summon all our powers of invective against one particular person or object of contempt.

Lucy Porter asked Dr Johnson if she was safe to trust what the reviewers of books told her: 'Infallibly, dear Lucy,' the Doctor told her, 'provided that you buy what they abuse, and never anything they praise.'

The Irish playwright, Brendan Behan, also had a disparaging opinion of theatrical reviewers: 'Critics are like eunuchs in a harem,' he said. 'They're there every night, they see it done every night, they see how it should be done every night, but they can't do it themselves.'

Religion has also come in for some scathing attacks from time to time. Sydney Smith, speaking with the benefit of first-hand experience, drew his well-known comparison between a sloth and the Church of England: 'What is most extraordinary is that he lives not upon the branches, but underneath them. He moves suspended, and passes his life in suspense – like a young clergyman distantly related to a bishop.'

On a broader front Bertrand Russell made this disparaging comment on the Holy Scriptures: 'So far as I can remember, there is not one word in the Gospels in praise of intelligence.'

The Restoration was not a period noted for its piety, but even Dr Robert South, a staunch supporter of the Royalist cause, drew the line at flagrant disrespect for the holy offices of the Church. Preaching on one occasion to Charles II and several members of his court, he noticed that some of them were dozing off during his sermon. Breaking off his address, he singled out one of the offenders and called to him: 'Lord Lauderdale, let me entreat you, rouse yourself; you snore so loud that you will wake the King.'

There is another lovely story that has nothing to do with obloquy, but which is very amusing, about the Revd Tatham, a fellow of Lincoln College, Oxford. He was renowned for preaching long sermons and, after one three-hour marathon, the only person left in the church was found to have quietly died.

Nations have always had pretty caustic things to say about one another, but Ken Tynan's damning condemnation of the Common Market cut across national frontiers, with its pervading prophecy of doom: 'I do not see the EEC as a great love affair. It is more like nine middle-aged couples with failing marriages meeting at a Brussels hotel for a group grope.'

It was Dean Acheson who observed of the British that we had lost an Empire but not yet found a role; and recent years have reflected a certain introspection and self-criticism. Challenging one of the bastions of English society, Lord Mancroft attempted to explain part of the national problem thus: 'Cricket is a game which the English, not being a spirited people, have invented to give themselves some conception of eternity.'

Speaking from the lower chamber of Parliament, Edward Heath once said of the opposite side of the House: 'I do not often attack the Labour Party. They do it so well themselves.'

During his time as Chancellor of the Exchequer, Denis Healey delivered a splendid put-down to Sir Geoffrey Howe, who had just finished denouncing the government's economic policy. Rising to his feet, the Chancellor told the house that he felt as if he had been 'savaged by a dead sheep'.

In the world of theatre, sardonic dismissals are part and parcel of the working atmosphere. It is a bit like the law of the jungle, the survival of the fittest, except that in this jungle it helps to be a rhinoceros with a very thick hide. When Coral Browne was asked about acting with her latest leading man, she replied: 'Fine, if you like acting with two and a half tons of condemned veal.'

Oscar Wilde had scant regard for the playwright who (with Pinero) has been named as the dramatist who restored reality to the English stage after nearly a hundred years of eclipse: 'The first rule for a young playwright to follow is not to write like Henry Arthur Jones ... The second and third rules are the same.'

'If heaven is going to be filled with people like Keir Hardie'

Pique

...

In a letter to a newspaper Valerie Eliot once told a story about her husband T. S. getting into a taxi, which is a delightful example of mild pique. Before driving off the cabbie slid back the glass window and said:

'T. S. Eliot, ain't it?' and T. S. replied:

'Er, yes, I didn't think that you'd recognise me.'

'Oh, I recognise you all right, I have 'em all in my cab. Who'd you think I had in yesterday, eh? Bertrand Russell, greatest philosopher in the western world, right?'

'Yes, I suppose so.'

'I said to him, Bertie, what's it all about then? And do you know, the twit couldn't tell me.'

...

Right at the other end of the emotional spectrum are the dying words reputedly spoken by one of the conspirators in the Gunpowder Plot, Sir Everard Digby, who was hanged, drawn and quartered. As the executioner pulled out his heart crying: 'Behold the heart of a traitor', eye-witnesses claim that Sir Everard cried back: 'Thou liest.'

Old age and questions about old age have frequently aroused resentment and hurt pride amongst those in the twilight of their years. The German Chancellor, Konrad Adenauer, developed a heavy cold when he was in his late eighties, which had to be treated by his doctor.

'I'm not a miracle worker, you know,' said the doctor. 'I can't succeed in making you younger.'

'I'm not asking you to,' replied Adenauer, 'as long as you succeed in making me older.'

Robert Benchley felt less inclined to speed the ageing process. At a Hollywood party, to which he arrived somewhat earlier than the majority of the guests, he found considerable satisfaction in being the only real ladies' man present. That was until the arrival of a brace of matinée idols and the gradual ebbing away of the girls who had been talking to him.

'Now, that's my idea of real he-men,' one of them said as she moved off.

'He-men,' scoffed Benchley. 'I'll bet the hair of their combined chests wouldn't make a wig for a grape.'

When Sir Winston Churchill was seventy-five he was asked whether he had any fear of death. 'I am ready to meet my Maker,' he told the questioner. 'But whether my Maker is prepared for the great ordeal of meeting me is another matter.'

Much earlier in his political career, but still with an eye towards the afterlife, Churchill was told by an ardent admirer of Keir Hardie's: 'He is not a great politician, but he will be in heaven before you or me, Winston.' To which Churchill replied: 'If heaven is going to be filled with people like Hardie, well the Almighty can have them to himself.'

When the ashes of Bonar Law were laid to rest in Westminster Abbey, Asquith expressed the widely held opinion of the late Premier, when he noted:

'It is fitting that we should have buried the Unknown Prime Minister by the side of the Unknown Soldier.'

Someone who was foolish enough to ask Lorenzo de Medici, on his deathbed, how he was enjoying his food, received the reply: 'As a dying man always does.'

Towards the end of her life Lady Strachey became very deaf and had to be read to in a loud voice. Hester Chapman was a frequent guest at the Strachey household in Bloomsbury. She told me once that as a young girl she used to read aloud to the rather deaf dowager. She bawled:

'I won't bother with the chapter headings, Lady Strachey,' and the latter replied mournfully:

'They're the only bits I like.'

There is a charming story about Lytton Strachey which I have always enjoyed. For some reason his Rolls-Royce simply refused to start and there was nothing anyone could do to make it. Realising that repair was impossible, Lytton said in that high-pitched voice of his: 'We'll have to turn it into a summer-house.'

Sir Winston's father, Lord Randolph Churchill, who had been Chancellor of the Exchequer in 1886, in later life used to comment with some feeling about decimal points: 'I never could work out what those damned dots meant.'

•••

Pique is an emotion ever-present in show business. Fashions change and there is always the possibility that people will say: 'We want some other kind of acting, we don't want your kind any more', reminding us that the theatre can be extraordinarily ephemeral. Indeed, the Lisson Grove Labour Exchange is known for its preponderance of celebrated stage names.

•••

Luckily, I have always had other strings to my bow. Apart from films, television and the odd bit of writing, radio has always stood me in good stead, and it is the medium where vocal dexterity lends enormous scope to characterisation. Indeed, in *Hancock's Half Hour*, my nasal whining of 'No, stop messin' about' became enormously popular. But only in the theatre have I been able to work with writers like Joe Orton, Charles Laurence, Robert Bolt, Mervyn Peake and Trevor Baxter, all of whom gave me the chance to create new roles. Acting something for the first time is a rare privilege because people cannot say, 'Well, we've seen so-and-so's Hamlet, let's see yours.' You're on virgin territory and therefore incomparable.

I have never had much cause to feel pique, though admittedly there are times when I have felt resentful and exploded, 'Nowadays, only the amateur can afford to be a professional.' One such outburst on radio prompted many listeners to write telling me to mind my manners and I endeavoured to reply in contrite fashion, remembering my mother's advice, 'Don't bite the hand that feeds you'. Though I'm not too sure about that, now the radio licence is free!

It was radio that gave me the chance to work with that singular Welsh comedian, Harry Secombe, who took over Tony Hancock's role in *Hancock's Half Hour* when the star was ill, triumphantly playing all the lines as to the manner born and not missing one of the laughs. When the Continuity Announcer said, 'This is the BBC Home Service', I always remember Harry screaming from behind him, 'And serve you right.' It left me and the audience convulsed. He has had a varied career, always observing the contemporary scene with an unjaundiced, but not totally uncritical eye. Some of his cracks are very pungent: 'These days a star is anyone who can hold a microphone. A super-star is someone who has shaken hands with Lew Grade, and a super-super-star is someone who has refused to shake hands with Lew Grade.' (Which reminds me of Adlai Stevenson's observation about election canvassing: 'You have to kiss an awful lot of babies and shake an awful lot of hands and you sometimes wonder what they've shaken before.')

Noël Coward said to a friend after the filming of *Design for Living* in Hollywood: 'I'm told that there are three of my original lines left in the film – such original ones as "Pass the mustard".' On the other hand, when a friend commiserated with Emlyn Williams over the cinema version of one of his plays and told him: 'There was this daft line: "You have one twisted foot but the Venus de Milo was mutilated too"! Can you imagine a more banal line?', he was told, 'Yes, I wrote it.'

I am constantly piqued by the general decline of literacy. A professor at one university averred: 'The rising tide of illiteracy is not only bringing in the water, it's bringing in the sewage as well.' He said that out of twenty graduates, there was not one who could tell him the angle in a semi-circle. If we look at the educational system today, we find that the money spent on new universities, technical colleges and universities has not produced higher standards. All these vast schemes designed for a literate population have in fact resulted in increasing illiteracy. The errors abound. During a television interview, I heard the leader of a trade union saying: 'The offer of the employers is derisory. I recline. I must recline. I have no option but to recline.' Then there was President Ford on television avowing to the American people: 'I believe in the Protestant ethnic', and arousing no perceptible derision. So many of the mistakes are ignored, doubtless because most of the time the half-educated are talking to the uneducated.

I left school when I was fourteen, becoming an apprentice draughts-man at Stanford's Geographical Institute in Long Acre, the cartographers that held the Royal warrant. The draughtsmen were cultivated and fluent, and certainly knew how to speak English. When I was showing off there about my social activities, I once said I was going to a dinner party and one of them corrected me drily: 'A dinner or a party.' One of their youthful employees had to deliver some estate maps to the then Poet Laureate, John Masefield.

'Here are your maps, Mr Masefield,' he said.

'You will address me as Dr Masefield,' he was told curtly.

And on returning to the drawing office, he informed the head draughtsman, who nodded sagely:

'Ah, like the German fashion. They are always meticulous about titles. They say: "Herr Doktor", not just "Doktor", "Herr".'

'Oh, no,' said the lad, 'he didn't have any hair.'

Hermione Gingold started working on the stage at a young age, like many actresses in the early part of the twentieth century. In fact she made her first appearance when she was eleven. She did not appear to suffer from any lack of formal education. Though, as she once remarked bitterly, there was no need to move far beyond the rudiments of elementary study: 'I got all the schooling any actress needs. That is, I learned to write enough to sign contracts.'

Then there are those occasions of bitter personal experience that engender grudges. When Oscar Wilde was released from prison and went to live in France he used to speak feelingly about his incarceration: 'If England treats her criminals the way she treated me, she doesn't deserve to have any.'

George Villiers, the notorious second Duke of Buckingham, whom Pope described as 'this Lord of useless thousands', was asked by a friend to use his influence at court to intercede on his behalf with Charles II, adding that he had no one to rely on but God and His Grace: 'Then,' said Villiers, 'your condition is desperate; you could not have named any two beings who have less interest at court.'

Sir Thomas Beecham answered a friend's enquiry as to whether he had been staying at a particular stately home: 'Yes, I spent a month down there last weekend.'

Dr Johnson suffered similarly whenever he was in company with the dramatist Oliver Goldsmith. After one evening spent listening to the playwright holding forth for hours on end, Johnson remarked: 'The misfortune of Goldsmith in conversation is this: he goes on without knowing how he is to get off.'

Resentment can easily be aroused in the course of a conversation, provoking some very sour rebuffs. Dr Erasmus Darwin, grandfather of the great anthropologist, suffered from a severe speech impediment. He was asked on one occasion whether he found his stammering inconvenient: 'No, sir,' he replied, 'it gives me time for reflection, and saves me from answering impertinent questions.

F. E. Smith, later Lord Birkenhead, was invited to give the annual address at a livery company dinner. His host rose to his feet and said: 'I

now call upon F. E. Smith, who needs no introduction from me ...',
whereupon he proceeded to give the most boring introduction imagin-
able. F. E. was fuming because he was the one who had been invited to
speak, and this old drear was droning on interminably, until he finally
announced: 'And I now call upon F. E. Smith for his address,' to which
F. E. replied: 'It's Grosvenor Square, and I'm going there right now.'

Pierre Monteux arrived from Europe at a hotel in New York,
exhausted by his journey and desperately in need of rest before his
concert the following evening. To his annoyance he was told by the
desk clerk that he could not stay at the hotel because it was restricted to
coloured people: 'But I am coloured,' Monteux protested, 'pink'.

Some surgeons are as funny as comedians

Quip

Oscar Wilde and James McNeill Whistler were dining together with friends one evening when Whistler made a particularly witty remark.

'I wish I had said that!' said Wilde, to which Whistler replied:

'You will, Oscar, you will.'

How many of us have shared Wilde's feelings and envied Whistler's instant quip? Brief, sarcastic, instantaneous repartee should be the aim of anyone seeking to emulate the famous wits of history. Of course Wilde has been the originator of countless similar comments himself, but it is amusing to see the evident rivalry that existed at the top of the league. Once a renowned society bore remarked to Wilde:

'I passed your house yesterday, Oscar.' Wilde replied:

'Thank you so much.'

J. M. Barrie did not like being pestered at home either. When a newspaper reporter knocked at his door unannounced and greeted him cheerily, 'Sir James Barrie, I presume?', Barrie replied, 'You do', and shut the door in his face.

After the death of the Poet Laureate, Alfred Lord Tennyson, there was great speculation about who would be appointed as his successor. Whenever the various candidates were discussed, no mention was ever made of Sir Lewis Morris, a popular poet whose works showed the clear influence of Tennyson. Complaining bitterly to Wilde about this neglect of his poetic talents, Lewis exclaimed:

'It is a conspiracy of silence against me – a conspiracy of silence! What should I do, Oscar?'

'Join it.'

When one of his clients appeared to be distinctly dissatisfied with his portrait, Whistler, far from making any apology, blamed the man for its defect.

'Do you call that a good piece of art?' asked the aggrieved subject.

'Well,' said Whistler, 'do you call yourself a good piece of Nature?'

Frank Harris, the journalist and 'adventurer', whose sensational autobiography *My Life and Loves* bears the rare distinction among such works of being banned as pornography, was a friend of both Wilde and Whistler, though his relationship with Wilde was always rather brittle. Entering the Café Royal one evening he was sighted by Wilde's notorious young friend, Lord Alfred Douglas, who called out across the restaurant:

'There goes Ancient Pistol.'

'Well roared, Bottom,' shouted back Whistler.

Before achieving fame as an artist, Whistler used to work in a large government department in Washington. As he was perpetually late for work, he was called in to his superior one day to be reprimanded. Instead of apologising, Whistler explained in a weary voice: 'It is not I that arrive too late. It is the office that opens too early.'

Charles Lamb took the same attitude when he was hauled over the coals by his head of department in India House.

'You arrive late, Mr Lamb,' his superior said.

'Yes,' replied Lamb, 'but see how early I leave.'

Quipping is also one of the most effective ways of insulting, or deflating those who presume to insult us. When the poet Edith Sitwell was in America she was accosted by one newspaper reporter who enquired aggressively:

'Why do you call yourself "Dame"?'

He was told soothingly: 'I don't. The Queen does.'

Douglas Jerrold was dining with friends on a meal of sheep's heads when one of the more oafish and offensive members of the company shouted enthusiastically:

'Well, sheep's heads for ever, say I!'

'There's egotism,' commented Jerrold.

The eighteenth-century mimic and actor Samuel Foote, after establishing himself as a master of farce, was regarded as an expert on comedy.

'Have you read my *Thoughts*?' Foote was asked by the author of some ridiculous book of that title.

'No,' replied Foote, 'I await the second volume.'

'And why is that, pray?'

'Because I have heard,' said Foote, 'that second thoughts were often best.'

Among Foote's contemporaries on the stage was the actress Louisa Lewis, who enjoyed a colourful and vigorous social life behind the scenes. To everyone's surprise she announced that she was getting married, which caused considerable comment.

'It is a very good match she has made,' said one of Foote's friends.

'And they say she made to her husband a full confession of all her past affairs,' commented another.

'What honesty she must have,' remarked a third.

'What courage!' – a fourth.

'What a memory!' added Foote.

The first Duke of Wellington was always punctilious and could never abide bad manners. As the Duke was getting into his carriage outside Apsley House, a stranger rushed forward and cried with undue familiarity, 'Mr Smith, I believe', and received the curt dismissal, 'If you believe that, you will believe anything.'

At a social gathering, a gushing female asked him apropos Waterloo, 'Tell me, my dear Duke, were you never surprised?'

Wellington replied wearily: 'Not half as much as I am now, Madam.'

Wellington treated gross exaggeration with similar terseness. With sub-ordinates his response was as crushing as his military victories, and his attitude towards his superiors was just as disdainful, though tempered with taciturn respect. George IV was boasting to the general once of his exploits as a young officer in the cavalry. They were both staying in Brighton and had taken a drive out to the Devil's Dyke, a precipitous hill, a few miles away. As they were admiring the scenery, the King enthusiastically told the Duke:

'I once galloped down that hill at the head of my regiment.'

'Very steep, sir,' Wellington replied.

Later, when Victoria was Queen, she told him of the exhaustive attempts to rid the Great Exhibition of the birds, which were causing such a nuisance within the huge glass structure. The remedies suggested by architects, ornithologists and engineers had all failed to solve the problem. What could the Duke suggest? 'Sparrow-hawks, Ma'am' was the laconic reply, which wasn't a put down; it was the solution.

George IV's sometime friend Beau Brummell had a fine line in deflationary comments as well. Asked once if he had ever seen such an appalling summer before, Brummell replied: 'Yes, last winter.'

Academics have always prided themselves on their quick-witted responses. Dr Home, President of Magdalen College, Oxford, was asked by an undergraduate for permission to go to Coventry. Granting his request Home told him: 'Better to go than be sent.'

I suppose it is only natural that the college that nurtured Oscar Wilde should attract men of similarly felicitous turns of phrase. Another of Magdalen's Presidents, Martin Routh, took a perverse delight in jokes. When one excitable fellow rushed up to him with the news that a member of the college had committed suicide, Routh said to him calmly: 'Pray, don't tell me who. Allow me to guess.'

I like the story, too, about the Magdalen President who developed the reputation for being a fearful snob. When it was announced that the son of the Mikado of Japan was to enter the college, an official from the Japanese embassy visited Oxford to make the necessary arrangements for the Crown Prince's arrival. The President, who was a stickler for protocol, asked how the new undergraduate should be addressed.

'At home it is customary to refer to him as the Son of God,' replied the diplomat sheepishly.

'That will present no problem,' replied the President, 'we are used to having the sons of distinguished men at Magdalen.'

The day after he became US Secretary of State, Henry Kissinger held a news conference. Taking questions at the end, he was asked: 'Do you prefer being called "Mr Secretary" or "Dr Secretary"?'

'I don't stand on protocol,' he answered. 'If you will just call me "Excellency", it will be OK.'

Winston Churchill was adept at the sharp rebuttal and must have been the envy of some of the mealy-mouthed politicians we have to suffer today. During the war Archbishop Lang expressed his concern to the Prime Minister that the precautions taken to protect Canterbury Cathedral from air-raids were totally inadequate.

'What will happen if there is a direct hit?' he demanded of Churchill.

'In that case, you will have to regard it as a divine summons.'

Actors and comedians are often expected to utter witty remarks at the drop of a hat, though I have never found actors particularly amusing. There are some who are, just as there are some surgeons and accountants who are, but they are the exception rather than the rule. I do not think any section of the community can be said to have a monopoly of wit. When we all gather for the Equity AGM, we don't hear much wit, alas. And we don't hear much literacy either. When actors achieve a reputation for wit, it is usually because they've acquired a repertoire of funny anecdotes.

I remember that marvellous raconteur, Ted Ray, comparing his mind with a file-index which helped him to remember his stories and relate them to other people, embellished with a little personal experience. It's because actors have retentive memories that they are able to spin out a good anecdote, but this has little to do with involuntary wit. W. C. Fields was an exception. When asked in his declining years why he was leafing through the Bible so assiduously, he boomed: 'Looking for loop-holes.'

Coral Browne was the exceptional actress who was really witty. She was taken backstage at the National Theatre – that splendid edifice which John Osborne dubbed 'Colditz-on-Thames' – and asked what she thought of the set for *Oedipus Rex*, the principal feature of which was a nineteen-foot-long golden phallus: 'Well,' said Coral, 'it's no one I know.'

Other actresses are celebrated for equally memorable remarks. When asked how many husbands she had had, Zsa Zsa Gabor replied: 'You mean apart from my own?'

One she failed to net was Porfirio Rubirosa, the diplomat-cum-playboy, who became the fifth husband of Barbara Hutton, heiress to the Woolworth fortune. On the day they married, Miss Gabor's picture appeared in the New York dailies, displaying the black eye she claimed he gave her when she refused to marry him. In spite of this, she wished the newly-weds 'all happiness' before telling reporters, 'I'm so glad he got married, or I probably would never have been able to get rid of him.'

•••

Elsa Lanchester once commented tartly of an aspiring ingénue: 'She looks as if butter wouldn't melt in her mouth ... or anywhere else.' And once on stage, when Mrs Patrick Campbell was faced with a would-be rival stringing out her lines with wild over-emphasis, she deflated the actress with the aside: 'Your eyes are so far apart, I think I'll have to take a taxi.' A cruel quip, perhaps, but one that reverberates in the memory and reminds me also of Michael Benthall directing the crowd scene in *Julius Caesar* at the Old Vic: 'I know I have asked you to avoid muttering "rhubarb, rhubarb" in your ad libs and say something realistic, but I don't want a repetition of Thursday night, when I heard a plebeian leave the Forum crying: "Taxi!"'

•••

Ridicule

'Very awkward for the cow'

Ridicule

Few malicious pleasures in life are as enjoyable as making others look and feel foolish. Satire may point out the errors of their ways, caustic wit may reap just revenge, but ridicule topples their plinths and reveals their feet of clay.

I have always been amused by the story of Tennyson's visit to Oxford where he received his honorary DCL. As he solemnly entered the Sheldonian Theatre wearing the magnificent gown of his new status, with his shoulder-length hair hanging in magnificent disorder, one of the spectators shouted from the gallery: 'Did your mother call you early, dear?'

Samuel Rogers, who was offered, but declined, the position of Poet Laureate on the death of Wordsworth, gained a reputation for his powers of conversation. He was holding forth at great length one day to a Scots lady on the virtue, in moments of danger, of having presence of mind. Instead of the expected approbation, all she said, when he had finished, was: 'I would rather have absence of body.'

As I have already said, Samuel Johnson had a singular ability to match his replies to the person he was addressing; he was seldom harsher than was necessary. It was Emerson who said: 'We have as many personalities as we have friends', which is both eloquent and truthful. When you think about it, you don't present the same persona to an ailing and elderly grandmother as you do to a friend in the four-ale bar. You adopt a kindly and solicitous tone, you tell the sort of stories that are appropriate, not the bawdy jokes you'd crack with contemporaries.

Johnson had a sort of sliding scale of sarcasm always suited to the occasion. He was at a reception once when he found himself surrounded by a group of admiring ladies, staring at him with undisguised wonder, rather than coy politeness. After suffering their silent gaze for a moment or two he said to them: 'Ladies, I am tame; you may stroke me.'

When Groucho Marx chose to be rude, however, he was so with devastating effect. Leaving a party one evening, he met his hostess at the door, and said: 'I've had a wonderful evening, but this wasn't it.'

The columnist and critic Alexander Woollcott would have approved. He never took kindly to being interrupted. At a college reunion, Woollcott was in mid-anecdote when a classmate slapped him on the back and boomed, 'Hello, Alex. You remember me, don't you?'

'I can't remember your name, but don't tell me,' Woollcott answered, before continuing his story.

Lilian Baylis could be equally deflating when it came to snuffing out romances between members of her theatrical companies, liaisons of which she generally disapproved. One day a young actor and actress presented themselves in front of her desk, hand in hand. There they stood nervously while she carried on writing. Then, scarcely lifting her gaze, she asked, 'Well, what is it?'

'Miss Baylis – we're in love,' announced the young actor, 'and ... and... we want to get married.'

'Go away,' she snapped. 'I haven't got time to listen to gossip.'

W. S. Gilbert probably took the same vindictive pleasure in going backstage to see an actor friend who had just given an execrable performance in an equally atrocious play. Bursting into the wretched actor's dressing-room, Gilbert exclaimed: 'My dear chap! Good isn't the word!'

Bernard Shaw was dining in a restaurant while being serenaded by an appalling orchestra. During the meal, the conductor noticed Shaw and sent a message to him asking if there was anything he would like them to play next. He replied in one word: 'Dominoes.'

Naturally it required the stature and reputation of someone like Shaw to carry off such a searing rebuttal, but then the conductor would never have asked a nonentity in the first place.

Whistler fell into the same category of pre-eminence, and those who courted his favour invariably courted disaster. When a would-be philanthropist and self-styled patron of the arts was thinking of bequeathing some of his most cherished paintings to an institution, he asked for Whistler's advice and he was told: 'I should leave them to an asylum for the blind.'

While on a visit to France, Whistler came across an Englishman in a restaurant, who was having some difficulty in making himself understood.

'May I help?' Whistler enquired genially, only to receive the gruff reply from the man that he could manage perfectly well on his own. 'I fancied contrary just now,' said Whistler, 'when I heard you desire the waiter bring you a pair of stairs.'

One occasion when Whistler hit national headlines was the famous Ruskin trial. Ruskin bitterly attacked Whistler's exhibits in the Grosvenor Gallery exhibition of 1877 and went as far as accusing him of 'flinging a pot of paint in the public's face', which led Whistler to take him to court for libel. During his cross-examination Whistler excelled himself in mocking Ruskin's counsel, Sir John Holker. Holker asked him:

'Now Mr Whistler. Can you tell me how long it took to knock off that nocturne?'

To which Whistler replied, after some jibbing at the term 'knock off':
'...well as I remember, about a day... I had better say, therefore, that I

was two days at work on it.'

'...the labour of two days, then, is that for which you ask two hundred guineas?'

'No,' answered Whistler. 'I ask it for the knowledge of a lifetime.'

Whistler won the case and was awarded damages – a farthing.

George Stephenson, the father of modern railways, adopted the same type of defence at the public hearing convened to look into the proposed construction of the Liverpool to Manchester railway. One of the opponents of the scheme asked Stephenson:

'Suppose, now, that a cow were to stray upon the line and get in the way of the engine, would not that, you think, be a very awkward circumstance?'

'Yes,' answered Stephenson, 'very awkward for the cow.'

Shortly before his death Sir Winston Churchill gave an interview to an eager cub reporter. As his time drew to an end the young man expressed his thanks and asked:

'I wonder if I might be able to interview you again next year.'

'I see no reason why you shouldn't,' Churchill replied. 'You appear to be a healthy enough young man, and will probably survive until then.'

Sir Thomas Beecham had a quixotic talent for making people feel stupid. He told one orchestral player who was having problems with the tempo: 'We cannot expect you to be with us all the time, but perhaps you would be kind enough to keep in touch now and again.'

Lord Ellenborough was presiding over a court case when an incompetent young barrister, shaking with nerves, addressed the court for the first time:

'My lord, my unfortunate client... My lord, my unfortunate client... My lord, my...'

'Go on, sir, go on,' Ellenborough told him, 'as far as you have proceeded hitherto the court is entirely with you.'

The French comic novelist, Tristan Bernard, went to pay a visit to a friend who lived at the top of a tall Parisian tenement. Half-way up he found the stairs blocked by a grandfather clock that one of the residents was trying to manoeuvre single-handed, but had only succeeded in jamming on one of the landings. After watching the man's vain, perspiring efforts to shift the obstruction for a couple of minutes, Bernard asked him: 'Excuse me, but wouldn't it be easier to wear a wristwatch?'

Noël Coward had an amusing way of pricking the bubble of pretension. Once he received a letter from a very pompous American, which began:
'From the desk of...'
Coward replied: 'Dear desk of...'

The reception for Yuri Gagarin, on his visit to London after becoming the first man to fly in space, was far more effusive than most commentators had expected. Harold Macmillan, however, remained impassive when a friend asked him excitedly what he thought of the cosmonaut's greeting. He only ventured the comment: 'It would have been twice as bad if they had sent the dog.'

Not long after the end of the Second World War, Clement Atlee presided over a meeting of the Parliamentary Labour Party which contained an item on the agenda about the atom bomb. This was an awe-inspiring subject and the MP Harold Davies rose to the occasion, delivering an emotional and powerful speech which brought cheers of approval from his colleagues when he sat down.
Atlee sat impassively as the cheering died away and then commented crisply:
'Yes, Harold, that is something we'll have to watch. Next business.'

I remember hearing of a conversation overheard by Sir Basil Blackwell when he was an undergraduate. Two undergraduates passed him on the way back from a formal dinner and he heard one say to the other:

'The conversation was rather precious wasn't it?'

'Yes,' said his friend, 'but I fancy I kept my end up.'

'Oh, indeed; but if you don't mind my mentioning it, Botticelli isn't a wine.'

'Isn't it?'

'My dear chap, it's a cheese.'

One of my favourite satirical rhymes comes from Dorothy Parker. It should be read effusively until the fourth line, when the voice should become metallic:

Life is a glorious cycle of song,
A medley of extemporania;
And love is a thing that can never go wrong,
And I am Marie of Romania.

Scorn

'Get out of my light'

Scorn, like ridicule, can be immensely satisfying, as long as one is the giver and not the receiver. Skilled practitioners uses their art to rise haughtily above their victims, crushing them beneath the mass of their disdain.

When Spencer Tracy was being harangued by an enormously enthusiastic method actor, the man told him that he should go to the Strasberg Studio to learn to act. 'Method acting,' the man assured him, was the coming thing, it would give him an entirely new slant on the art of acting. All Tracy said in reply was: 'I'm too old, I'm too tired and I'm too talented to care.'

Another actor attempted to impress Beerbohm Tree by telling him that he had been on the stage for forty-five years. 'Really, forty-five years!' said Tree. 'Almost a lifetime, eh? Any experience?'

One of the older members of the Garrick Club, who was a proverbial bore and a dreadful snob, told Tree once:

'When I joined, all the members were gentlemen.'

'I wonder why they left?' asked Tree.

The actor and director Robert Atkins was notorious for stinging rebukes, though once in a while the tables were turned. Atkins was walking beside the docks in Bristol one day when he and his companion came alongside a four-masted sailing ship. 'Look at her,' mused Atkins. 'That beautiful barque has sailed the seven seas bringing us tea from Ceylon, jewels from India, silks from China, spices from Samarkand and there she lies about to depart at our behest.

'Sailor – whither sailest thou?' he called to one of the deck-hands.

Hardly bothering to look in Atkins' direction the man called back, 'Fuck off!'

Oscar Wilde held a very contemptuous view of many of his literary peers. Criticising the elliptic mannerisms of the novelist George Meredith, he was able to kill two birds with one stone: 'Meredith is a prose Browning,' he said, 'and so is Browning.'

He could be deliberately rude to people he despised. He once replied to a dinner invitation sent by a couple whom he detested, saying that he was 'unable to accept owing to a subsequent engagement'.

Although Beau Brummell died in penury, he was a man of exquisite taste and gracious living. His wardrobe, his diet and his palate were cultivated to appreciate the finest that money could buy, and whenever anything fell below his standards he never missed an opportunity of saying so. Dining once at a house in Hampshire, where the champagne was of a decidedly inferior quality, he waited for a lull in the conversation before calling loudly to the wine servant: 'John, give me some more of that cider, will you.'

One of the dangers of party-going is that you run the risk of becoming involved in a conversation where you find yourself slightly out of your depth. The consequences can be humiliating. Porson provides a vivid illustration of this. He was entertaining in Trinity one evening when the conversation centred on the voyages of Captain Cook. One of the guests, who had so far contributed nothing to the dialogue, anxiously asked Porson:

'Pray, was Cook killed on his first voyage?'

'I believe he was,' answered Porson, 'though he did not mind much, but immediately entered on a second.

In contrast Sydney Smith regarded the manifestation of too much knowledge as equally reprehensible. He said of one of the leading scholars of his day: 'He not only overflowed with learning but stood in slops.'

Impertinence and precocity were two follies that Whistler scorned, quite rightly. He was looking round a private gallery in London, when some pompous woman, recognising him, walked across to ask if a painting she had been studying was indecent: 'No, madam,' Whistler told her, 'but your question is.'

He was attending a dinner of famous artists in London, when a young man of no acknowledged talent began to make a nuisance of himself. Pontificating to the distinguished company on the theory of art, he had the impudence to contradict Whistler himself. There was a brief pause in which Whistler glared at the callow youth through his monocle, before asking: 'And whose son are you?'

Daniel François Esprit Auber, a much neglected genius of nineteenth-century French opera, was as scathing as Whistler in his opinion of musical parvenus. Asked to review a score written by a precocious composer which was filled with 'originality' that far exceeded his years, Auber observed: 'This boy will go far, when he has had less experience.'

There must be few figures in history, however, who rival Alexander the Great for precocity. Conqueror of the world and dead before he was thirty-three, he is probably unsurpassed in youthful ambition and attainment. Even Alexander, though, was slighted by the great Cynic philosopher, Diogenes, who eschewed even the very modest comforts of ancient Greek life and chose to live in a barrel. Knowing his reputation, Alexander presented himself at the mouth of the barrel one morning and asked the great philosopher if he could be of some service to him. 'Yes,' Diogenes told him. 'I should like you to get out of my light.'

During the most critical period of the Napoleonic wars, when the country was on the verge of being attacked, William Pitt received one offer of national assistance in a manner worthy of Diogenes himself. A large body of men sent a letter to the Prime Minister in which they expressed their willingness to serve in the Army against Napoleon subject to the condition that they should not be sent overseas. 'Except, I presume,' remarked Pitt sardonically to his private secretary, 'in case of invasion.'

I have little time for hypocrites who castigate actors for their insincerity, while displaying the same foible themselves. It's like the man who whips the coachman because the coachman whipped the horse. If they stopped to think, they'd realise that calling someone 'darling' or 'sweetie' is no more affected than asking a man, 'How's your wife?' when you care precious little for him or his spouse. It all helps to oil the wheels of social intercourse. We must never confuse sincerity with truth, even when certain formulas tend to ossification.

• • •

Institutions often obfuscate original visions, and then we need the radical swipe of a reappraisal. Indeed, Lord Altrincham reflected this with his scornful dismissal of the Anglican attitude to confirmation: 'One of the sacraments of the Church of England – tends to be like a spiritual sheep-dip.' The institution H. L. Mencken didn't like was the Rotary Club: 'The first Rotarian,' he observed, 'was the first man to call John the Baptist Jack.'

• • •

The scorn of one's professional colleagues can be the most damning of all. In the course of one of his many legal wrangles, F. E. Smith was asked by one judge:

'What do you suppose I am on the Bench for, Mr Smith?'

To which F. E. replied: 'It is not for me to attempt to fathom the inscrutable workings of Providence.'

Beecham could be as cutting with orchestral players when he chose to be. When he asked one principal oboe for an A to tune the orchestra, the man produced the note with a very wide vibrato. 'Gentlemen,' said Beecham to the rest of the orchestra, 'take your pick.'

Terseness

'I think it would be a very good idea'

Being nasty to someone doesn't require a giant intellect; any moron can be abusive. The distinguishing factor of the great wit is to be nasty with style. Concise, polished, refined insults have the same subtle superiority over coarse rudeness that wine-vinegar has over its country cousin made from malt. Courtiers and diplomats have often personified this gift of terseness. An American writer, Caskie Stinnet, described the diplomat as 'a person who can tell you to go to hell in such a way that you actually look forward to the trip'.

In the days when treason was more readily punishable, expressing a derogatory opinion about monarchy could be a difficult task. The politician John Wilkes used to claim that he 'so loved the King [George III] that he hoped never to see another'. So naturally it came as rather a surprise when he once proposed the King's health at a dinner attended by the Prince of Wales, his rival. The Prince asked Wilkes how long he had been so concerned with the perpetuation of his father's life, to which the MP replied: 'Since I had the honour of Your Royal Highness's acquaintance.'

At about the same period, in 1783, William Pitt the Younger visited George III at Windsor Castle to be appointed as Prime Minister. Astonished by Pitt's age – he was only twenty-four – George III was doubtful about his ability to run the country.

'You're very young, Mr Pitt,' muttered the King, to which Pitt replied: 'I think we can rely on time to remedy that, sire.'

Royalty have the disconcerting habit of frequently asking awkward questions and putting their subjects on the spot when they cannot answer them. The poet Edmund Waller, however, was able to extricate himself with consummate panache from an even more embarrassing question than that asked of Wilkes by the Prince of Wales. Charles II demanded of Waller one day why his panegyric on Cromwell as Lord

Protector was so much better than the poem he had written to celebrate the King's restoration. 'Please, Your Majesty,' explained Waller, 'we poets always excel in fiction.'

The novelist Henry Fielding was related to the Earl of Denbigh, whose family had the same name, though spelt in a different way. The Earl tackled the novelist on one occasion and asked him to explain why his name was spelt 'Fielding' while the Earl's family name was spelt 'Feilding'.

'I cannot tell, my lord,' apologised *Fielding*, 'except it be that my branch of the family were the first that knew how to spell.'

I have always been intrigued by the way that statesmen and leading international figures talk and write when they are putting people in their place. Asked for his opinion of New York when he returned from a visit, Churchill answered in seven words: 'Newspapers too thick, lavatory paper too thin.'

That wonderfully unconventional statesman Mahatma Gandhi seemed to instil all the wisdom of the Orient in his wizened frame. I relish the reply he gave to the interviewer who asked him what he thought about Western civilisation: 'I think it would be a very good idea.'

Abraham Lincoln used to have a delightfully equivocal stock reply to publishers and writers who sent him countless copies of books, usually with notes attached asking him to read them. Lincoln would answer: 'Be sure that I shall lose no time in reading the book which you have sent me.'

Sir Maurice Bowra acquired the reputation of being a prodigious reader by using a very similar principle. He always advised people to follow his own practice: 'Acknowledge the receipt of books and articles *immediately* they are sent, then there'll be no need to read them.'

If ever he did read a book, or start a book which he found out to be worse than his judgement had led him to believe, Bowra had a stock phrase which soon became dreaded in the Senior Common Rooms of Oxford. Whenever he was asked whether he had read one of these offending volumes, Bowra would answer that it was: 'The sort of book that once put down you can't pick up again.'

An important nineteenth-century figure in educational policy was the politician Robert Lowe, later Lord Sherbroke. Although he strongly opposed the exclusive study of classics in schools, he retained great respect for them as an academic discipline. Seen by many as a champion of their own ineptitude and idleness in the subject, Lowe reacted strongly against this. A friend who announced to him one day:

'I have the greatest contempt for Aristotle,' promptly received the answer:

'But not, I should imagine, that contempt which familiarity breeds.'

During the nine years in which Charles Dickens edited his magazine *Household Words*, he received work from many authors and poets in the hope that he would include something of theirs in his publication. Receiving a poem one day from a young man called Laman Blanchard, Dickens read it through. The piece had been given the title 'Orient Pearls at Random Strung', and when he had finished reading it, Dickens returned it to the poet with a note that read: 'Dear Blanchard, too much string. Yours, C. D.'

Telegrams have always been an ideal medium for brief, witty messages. Dorothy Parker was holidaying abroad when she heard that a friend had given birth, after an immodestly publicised pregnancy. She immediately sent her a telegram, saying: 'Many congratulations. I knew you had it in you.'

Calvin Coolidge was naturally a man of terse wit, whose humour tended towards the brief, rather than the polished repartee. Living with him must have been a soul-destroying ordeal if this story is anything to go by. Coolidge had been to church alone. When he came home his wife asked him what the sermon had been about.

'Sin,' he replied.

'What did the preacher have to say about sin, then?' she said, plunging the President into deep thought for some minutes, until he replied at last:

'He's against it.'

On another occasion Coolidge was seated next to a very attractive guest at one of the White House banquets. Summoning up all her courage, the young lady said sweetly:

'Mr President, I have a wager with some of my friends that I can make you say at least three words to me during the course of this evening.'

'You lose,' grunted Coolidge, and stayed mute for the rest of the evening.

The exchanges between those who are never supposed to display their real feeling are always terribly amusing for onlookers, who relish the spectacle of two agile minds indulging in a sort of cerebral judo. I have always found clergymen particularly adept at this. Cardinal Vaughan found himself seated next to Hermann Adler, the Chief Rabbi, at an inter-denominational dinner.

'Now, Dr Adler,' he enquired, 'when may I have the pleasure of helping you to some ham?'

'At your Eminence's wedding,' was the reply.

Courts of law are frequently settings for exchanges like this.

'I have listened to you, Mr Smith, but I am none the wiser,' a judge told F. E. Smith.

'Possibly not, my lord,' he replied, 'but you are much better informed.'

The early seventeenth-century Chief Justice for Wales, Sir John Walton, was told in his declining years by a fellow judge on the western circuit:

'My lord, you are not merry.'

'Merry enough for a judge,' he replied.

Sir William Grant, a former Master of the Rolls, was one of those judges who would sit silently and patiently while evidence was presented in a trial. For two days he listened attentively to a complicated case which hinged on a particular interpretation of an Act of Parliament. Sir William allowed the barrister presenting the case all the time he needed to air his carefully constructed argument. Only when he had exhausted this did the judge allow himself to tell the jury:

'Gentlemen, the Act on which the pleading has been founded is repealed.'

Wit of this type is more commonly found in mature heads than in those filled with the dizzy fantasies of youth. A few years before his death in 1972, that wonderful French artist Maurice Chevalier, asked how he felt about growing old, answered: 'I prefer it to the alternative.'

Rumours of his own death eventually caught up with Mark Twain after they had been circulating for some time. Interviewed about them, the novelist said: 'The reports of my death have been much exaggerated.'

When Shaw was in his eighties he was asked for his opinion on youth and is supposed to have replied: 'I think that it is wasted on the young.'

One example of Shaw's spontaneous wit which I have always enjoyed is his reply to a beautiful woman's suggestion that they should have a child.

'Imagine, a child with my body and your brain!' she exclaimed.

'Yes,' said Shaw, 'but what if it had my body and your brain?'

Coral Browne favoured a robust approach in asserting herself in the 'battle of the sexes'. She was once lucky enough to hail the only free taxi outside the Haymarket Theatre when she left rehearsals in pouring rain. On the other side of the road the same taxi was hailed by a respectable young man, who had failed to notice Coral Browne, and who now ran across the street, opened a door and said to the driver: 'Mansion House, please.'

'Sorry – I saw the lady first,' he was told.

With no sight of a lady on the rainswept street, the man asked, 'What lady?'

From the dark recess of the taxi, where she sat wrapped in a fur coat, Coral Browne tapped her chest and said:

'This fucking lady!'

Upstaging

'The Queen never takes any notice . . .'

Upstaging

The principles of upstaging and one-upmanship are very similar, they both aim to gain the upper hand over others in order to establish or confirm one's own superiority. When a bumptious actor boasted to me: 'I've actually got into *Who's Who in the Theatre*. Are you in *Who's Who in the Theatre*?' I couldn't resist saying: 'I'm not only in *Who's Who in the Theatre*, I'm in *Who's Who*.'

Shaw, who was a genius at doing this, used to say: 'I occasionally swank a little because people like it: a modest man is such a nuisance.' He once had the satisfaction of making his presence felt on the other side of the world by following this maxim. A company in New Zealand was performing *Saint Joan* on a tour of the country. In these days the transport system was still in its infancy and they were always dashing from the theatre to the station to catch the train that would take them to their next touring date. At one town they found that the only way in which they were going to catch their train on time was by cutting the play, since there was not enough time to perform it in its entirety. So they wired Shaw for permission to cut the epilogue. The cable they got back read: 'Permission to cut epilogue granted provided you perform it on train.' It was probably the only time the Maid of Orleans learned of her canonisation on a sleeper to Auckland.

There is another story of Shaw gaining the upper hand, this time in the West End. During one of his productions the leading man was persuaded to act as spokesman for the cast in complaining about the leading lady, who was always drunk on stage. 'Yes, yes, I know,' said Shaw, 'but I would rather have her drunk in the part than any other actress sober.'

In fact that story is very like one attributed to Abraham Lincoln. At the outbreak of the Civil War an influential group of Lincoln's ministers were determined to oppose his choice of Ulysses S. Grant as Commander-in-Chief of the Union Army. They told the President that Grant was no gentleman, but Lincoln countered them by pointing out that the other commanders might be too gentlemanly to win the war.

'But Grant drinks,' they persisted.

'Then tell me the name of his blend. I'll send some casks to the other generals. Grant gets victories.'

On the stage, directors have frequently found it necessary to assert themselves, especially when dealing with senior members of the cast. During the rehearsals for the *Hay Fever* production at the National, Noël Coward became very irritated with Dame Edith Evans, who was continually getting her lines wrong.

'Edith,' he protested, 'this is not good enough. You don't know your lines.'

'It's ridiculous,' she said, 'because this morning I said them over and over to myself, and I knew them backwards.'

'That's how you're saying them, dear, backwards.'

There was a marvellous example of Coward's spontaneous wit in the same production, also connected with Edith Evans. Somewhere in the play Judith Bliss says to Sandy: 'On a clear day you can see Marlow.' But Dame Edith kept saying, 'On a fine day...' This infuriated Coward so much that he finally shouted from the stalls: 'On a *clear* day you can see Marlow – and Beaumont and Fletcher.'

Peter Ustinov got just as fed up with a tiresome method actor in one of his productions and in the end screamed at the man: 'Don't just do something – stand there.'

J. M. Barrie shared his exasperation while rehearsing *Quality Street*. Things were going slowly, largely owing to a young actor who kept stopping to seek reassurance for every move and line. In the end Barrie could take no more and when the young man asked for yet another small point of direction, he was told:

'I should like you to convey when you are acting that the man you portray has a brother in Shropshire who drinks port.'

There are some eventualities, however, that even the most proficient director cannot guard against. After the first night, there is very little you can do about actors who forget their lines or paraphrase the author. Some artists complain that Shaw's lines are difficult to learn, though I have never found them more difficult than Somerset Maugham. Admittedly there tends to be a lot of them, but once they are captured, you don't lose them. There is an intrinsic rhythm and swell to his cadences which are hard to forget.

I played the Dauphin in the 1955 production of *Saint Joan*, in which the distinguished Irish actress Siobhan McKenna won the *Evening Standard* Award for her memorable performance in the title role. I remember one disastrous night in particular, when the Bishop forgot his lines in the middle of one of his long speeches. Instead of 'You stand alone, utterly alone...' he rambled on, mumbling, 'You're on your own, that's what you are. You're on your own...' In the end he had to ask for a prompt, but none was forthcoming, so he turned to the house and said: 'I'm very sorry, but this is an extremely difficult play to learn, so you'll have to bear with us', whereupon he departed to the prompt corner and brought the script back on with him. The sight of a fourteenth-century bishop struggling with twentieth-century hornrims astonished the audience as much as the rest of the cast.

Of course, there's more than one way of forgetting your lines. Drink can consign them to oblivion. There was a splendid example of this on stage during a production of *Richard II* many years ago. John of Gaunt came staggering on at the opening of the play and then lurched drunkenly about the stage without saying anything to the King at all. The audience became restless and started rustling their programmes, trying to find out who on earth was playing the part. Hearing this noise the actor made his way unsteadily to the front of the stage and said: 'If you think I'm drunk, wait until you see the Duke of Buckingham.'

Perhaps the ultimate disaster for any actor happened to Wilfred Lawson at a matinée. Having lunch in a pub near the theatre, he had run into Richard Burton and had invited him to see the show in the afternoon. As he was not on stage at the opening, Lawson offered to sit in the circle with Burton to begin with. The play had been running for about twenty minutes, when Burton began to get a bit anxious and thought that perhaps Lawson ought to get made-up and change into his costume. But he did not seem in a hurry to leave, and sat watching enthralled. After a few more minutes, he tapped Burton on the shoulder: 'This is the good bit,' he whispered. 'This is where I come on.'

• • •

Richard also told of the incident when Esmé Percy's glass eye fell out during *The Lady's Not For Burning*, landing in the folds of the young actor's doublet. Esmé hissed: 'Give it back!' and Richard recorded: 'It was the first time anyone literally had their eye on me.'

• • •

When mishaps on stage are not of their own making, many actors show great presence of mind, rising above the situation and carrying off the emergency with suavity and aplomb. David Tomlinson once extinguished a fire on stage with a syphon of soda-water, and the great Czech tenor, Leo Slezak, succeeded in overcoming a disaster at the finale of *Lohengrin*. After singing his farewell he made his way majestically to the back of the stage to depart in the boat drawn by the swan. However, owing to a fatal error in timing, the boat set off before Slezak had time to step on board. Stranded but composed he turned to the audience saying: 'Tell me, what time is the next swan?'

It is not unknown, of course, for an audience to have the last word. Peter Dews, the director of the 1969 production of *Antony and Cleopatra* at Chichester, overheard a lady leaving the auditorium after one performance saying: 'Yes, and the funny thing is, exactly the same thing happened to Monica.' And when the Lunts were appearing in Dürrenmatt's *The Visit* at Brighton, one lady leaving the matinée was heard confiding to a companion, 'Course, you can tell her age when you get to the *hands*.' I've overheard some telling remarks myself. During *Macbeth* at the Royal Court, the lady seated in front of me leaned forward to her friend braying: 'So you see how one *lie* leads on to another *lie*!'

An equally engaging audience comment was overheard when Sarah Bernhardt was playing Cleopatra in London in 1892. She concluded her performance with a magnificent *coup de théâtre* that invariably brought the house to its feet in a tumultuous standing ovation. She ended her performance by wrecking her palace and then collapsing dramatically among the debris that littered the scene. After the applause had died away, an elderly lady in the stalls was heard remarking to her companion: 'How different, how very different from the home life of our own dear Queen.'

It is very gratifying to find out that 'our own dear Queen' is able to have a dig at people now and again. There is a lovely story about a meeting she had with Mrs Thatcher at one of their regular weekly audiences. The Prime Minister found to her consternation that they were both wearing the same dress. She decided that in future she would have to find out in advance what the Queen was wearing. But when one of her staff rang the Palace to arrange this he was told that it would be quite unnecessary. 'You see,' explained the Palace spokesman, 'the Queen never takes any notice of what her visitors are wearing.'

Not long before the 1979 general election, Norman St John-Stevas left a Shadow cabinet meeting early, explaining to his party leader that he had to attend a function.

'But Norman, I'm going as well,' reprimanded Mrs Thatcher, 'and I'm not leaving.'

'Ah, but Margaret,' said the Shadow Minister, 'it takes me so much longer to change than you.'

As the headmaster of Westminster School, Richard Busby, was giving King Charles II a tour of the school, he apologised for wearing his hat in the King's presence, but excused himself on the grounds that: '...it would not do for my boys to suppose that there existed in the world a greater man than Dr Busby.'

Another famous academic, of our time, Sir Maurice Bowra, has many stories attached to his name, many of them no doubt apocryphal. The one which has always appealed to me concerns Parson's Pleasure, a swimming place on the River Cherwell, in Oxford, that was reserved exclusively for nude male bathing. Bowra and a group of other dons were taking a dip there one afternoon, when a punt full of women missed the main stream and came drifting through the swimming area. All the men grabbed their towels and held them round their waists, but Bowra put his over his head.

'Why on earth did you do that?' one of them asked him.

'I don't know about you gentlemen,' replied Bowra, 'but in Oxford I'm known by my face.'

Of all the late nineteenth-century wits, I think Whistler ranks as the most persistent upstager. His ego was undaunted, even at an early age. His West Point career was ended by his failure to pass the exam in military history. Called before the board of examiners for a viva, he appalled them by his ignorance:

'What! You don't know the date of the battle of Buena Vista?' one of them cried, flabbergasted. 'Suppose you went out to dinner and the company began to talk about the Mexican War and you, a West Point man, were asked the date of this battle, what would you do?'

'I should refuse to associate with people who could talk of such things at dinner,' Whistler replied.

That reminds me of the time when Lytton Strachey was brought before a military tribunal investigating his conscientious objection to military service. One grizzled veteran leaned forward and asked: 'What would you do if a German tried to rape your own sister?' which elicited the reply: 'I should try to interpose myself between them.'

In later life Whistler observed sarcastically: 'If other people are going to talk, conversation becomes impossible.' When a woman commented that the view of the Thames that she had just seen reminded her exactly of his series of paintings, Whistler told her: 'Yes, madam. Nature is creeping up.' Asked by another admirer if his genius was hereditary, he replied: 'I cannot say. Heaven has granted me no offspring.'

A rather unexpected, but nonetheless delightful example of upstaging was the reply from the late Cardinal Heenan, in the witness box on one occasion.

'You are probably the most intelligent man in England,' said the barrister.

'Yes, I suppose you could say that.'

Vitriol

. . . like the Levantines, they are not outraged

Vitriol

The finest example of vitriol that I know came from Orson Welles. He had just finished playing Othello before a matinée audience that was composed entirely of school-children. They were packed in the gallery and the rest of the auditorium was almost empty. The children had attended the play because it was part of their examination syllabus. As the curtain was held because the children clapped so enthusiastically, Orson was compelled to come forward and make a speech: 'I would just like to mention Robert Houdin who in the fourteenth century invented the vanishing bird-cage trick and the theatre matinée – may he rot and perish. Good afternoon.' As one who has suffered endless matinées, I sympathise with him entirely. They are truly dispiriting experiences.

Class distinction has often caused vitriolic malevolence. Nothing is more provoking to some people than the accent of the governing classes. Luckily, the theatre has enabled me to iron out some of my Cockneyisms, but I am probably more at home on the lower deck of a cruise ship than in the First Class lounge, because the upper classes are more inhibited by nature. They are more formal. Perhaps it stems from the tradition of being served and not talking in front of the servants, or it may be that the very idea of formality itself appeals to them. The working classes, on the other hand, have no such qualms. If one does eructate during a meal, they, like the Levantines, are not outraged.

Where class division does exist, the malice bred from misunderstanding can achieve frightening proportions. Lord Curzon was as famous for his arrogance as he was for his unbending deportment. While he was visiting the trenches during the Great War he came across some troops bathing and remarked to his aide: 'I never knew the lower classes had such white skins.'

President Truman astutely summed up the attitude of self-complacency that pervades the industrial world today, as much as it did in the thirties, in the bitter definition: 'It's a recession when your neighbour loses his job: it's a depression when you lose yours.'

Rivalry between the armed services has often been conducted in terms of bitter jealousy. During the war Churchill had to reprimand a member of the Admiralty top brass, who had complained that the Senior Service was not being allowed to play its rightful role in the war according to its great traditions. 'Well, Admiral,' Churchill told him, 'have you ever asked yourself what the traditions of the Royal Navy are? I will tell you in three words. Rum, sodomy and the lash.'

The Labour statesman Philip Snowden made an equally acrid comment on totalitarianism when he remarked once: 'There are no unemployed in Russia or in Dartmoor jail, and for the same reason.'

Vitriol among individuals takes many different forms. Between associates it can be the word of reproach like Fitzgerald's remark on Hemingway: 'Always willing to lend a helping hand to the one above him.'

It can take the form of the weary complaint, like Voltaire's comment on Diderot after he had spent an evening in the company of the incessant talker: 'An extraordinary man! There's only one art he doesn't understand – the art of dialogue.'

Then there is the public vitriol that characterises many political feuds. Roy Jenkins, when Home Secretary, once said of the leader of the Opposition: 'I am sure that Mr Heath thinks he is honest. But I wish he didn't have to have his friends say it so often.'

Self-administered vitriol can often be amusing. Lord George-Brown commented once: 'Most British statesmen have either drunk too much or womanised too much. I never fell into the second category.' Incidentally, I remember *The Times* remarking in an editorial: 'Lord George-Brown drunk is a better man than the Prime Minister sober.'

Rex Whistler left a friend's party rather the worse for wear, missed his footing as he tried to negotiate the stairs and arrived down in the hall in a bruised, undignified heap. As his host helped him to his feet, he asked tetchily who had designed the house.

'Norman Shaw' was the answer.

'I might have known it,' said Whistler. 'The damned teetotaller.'

Some particularly harsh things have been said about women in history, especially those who have not been blessed with radiant beauty. A courtier of King George III's was commenting to one of the royal household on the apparent improvement in Queen Charlotte Sophia's looks as she grew older. 'Yes,' said the chamberlain, 'I do think that the bloom of her ugliness is going off.'

Groucho Marx was attempting to remain unnoticed at a Hollywood party when he was accosted by a lady columnist who had neither tact nor beauty to commend her:

'Dear Mr Marx, we met at Mrs Finklestein's party. I'm sure you remember me?'

'I never forget a face, but in your case I'm willing to make an exception.'

From more recent times comes the story of the Great Train Robber, Ronnie Biggs, who managed to elude British justice after his escape from prison by taking refuge in Brazil. There he resisted extradition, claiming protected status under Brazilian law because his girlfriend, Ramona, was pregnant with their child. Back in the UK, Charmian Biggs, his estranged wife, was asked her opinion and told reporters:

'For a pregnant Brazilian girl, Ron's a prime catch.'

Dying men have occasionally had the presence of mind to say astonishingly trenchant and bitter things either before or during execution. One of the early Christian martyrs, St Lawrence, was roasted alive on a gridiron for refusing to hand over his church's treasures to the emperor. In the midst of his agony he turned to the judge who had sentenced him and said:

'*Assum est, versa et manduca.*'

('This side is well done; turn me over and eat.')

John Brown, the campaigner against slavery, whose name has been immortalised in the song, was asked on the scaffold whether he was tired.

'No,' he replied, 'but don't keep me waiting for longer than necessary.'

There are occasions when vitriol and malice fall completely flat. When a film director said to the leading member of a pop group:

'You know, you have Van Gogh's ear for music,' he received the grateful reply:

'Gee! Thanks!'

Edmund Wilson, the American essayist and critic, became so fed up with the stream of letters he received from people he didn't know asking for his advice and help with a range of disparate subjects that he printed a card to be sent in reply. It read: 'Edmund Wilson regrets that it is impossible for him to: read manuscripts, write articles or books to order, write forewords or introductions, make statements for publicity purposes, do any kind of editorial work, judge literary contests, give interviews, take part in writers' conferences, answer questionnaires, contribute to or take part in symposiums or panels of any kind, contribute manuscripts for sales, donate copies of his books to libraries, autograph works for strangers, allow his name to be used on letterheads, supply personal information about himself, supply opinions on literary or other subjects.'

Although this stemmed the flow of unwanted correspondence, it was only partially successful: in its place he began getting letters from people wanting copies of the card.

Wordplay

How very singular!

All jokes fall into one of three categories: situations, relationships and linguistics. The pun comes under the last heading and it is one which has always given me pleasure. I have never shared the disparagement expressed by some about the pun. Few authors worth reading have ever scorned it. Whilst not being an inveterate punster, I do remember once hearing a discussion with a casting director about the difference between mulattos and creoles. Somebody asked: 'What is a half-caste?' and I said: 'Someone who has been promised the part.'

One of my real favourites is recorded by Charles Lamb from his Oxford days. An undergraduate was walking down the High in the early hours of the morning after a tipsy all-night party, when he suddenly came upon a poacher, surreptitiously creeping home as the dawn was rising. He had a couple of rabbits dangling from his coat pockets and the undergraduate quipped: 'Hello, is that your own hare, or is it a wig?'

(This calls to mind an occasion when the American attorney, Max Steuer, began his cross-examination of a witness. The man was a barber by trade, though when Steuer asked him what he did for a living, he told the court loftily that he was a 'tonsorial artist'. 'Isn't that splitting hairs?' enquired the attorney.)

Critics have always had a field day with puns. Caroline Lejeune, reviewing the film of *I Am a Camera*, the forerunner of *Cabaret*, wrote: 'Me no Leica.'

Alexander Woollcott noted of one performance he had attended: 'The audience strummed their catarrhs.'

The humour in puns can also help to save dreadfully embarrassing situations. Beatrice Lillie had the misfortune to have soup poured down her brand-new evening gown when she was dining at Buckingham Palace. For a moment there was a dreadful silence, before she saved the situation by rising to her feet and saying in mock anger to the unfortunate person: 'Never darken my Dior again.'

There have been punsters in most professions, all the great wits have punned at some time in their careers, and the stage has had no shortage of them, both on and off the boards.

• • •

W. S. Gilbert was rehearsing Henrietta Hodson in the lead of one of his plays. She was having difficulty with the blocking and Gilbert was becoming exasperated with her, when she accidentally missed her chair and sat down heavily on the stage. 'Very good! Very good!' he shouted from the stalls, 'I always knew you would make an impression on the stage one of these days.'

• • •

Jerome Kern was having similar difficulty with one of his cast in *Show Boat*. The actress had the irritating habit of rolling her R's.

'You want me to cr-r-ross the stage,' she said. 'How am I supposed to get acr-r-ross the stage?'

'Why don't you just roll on your R's?' suggested Kern.

Following the huge success of his novel *The Green Hat* in the mid-1920s, Michael Arlen visited America. Chicago was one of his destinations and he cut an impressive figure as he stepped from the train in a broad-brimmed hat and an overcoat with an impressive fur collar. One of the reporters waiting to greet him asked to what he attributed his success.

'*Per ardua ad astrakhan*,' replied the author.

A carefully chosen pun can be as malicious and cutting as any of the more orthodox acid drops. A television personality was telling his colleagues about the great demands that were made on his time, while they were getting ready to record a programme. He was going on about all the charities he had been asked to assist and about all the places where he had been invited to go and speak, and he finished off the catalogue by announcing that he had just been invited to become President of his local rifle association. 'Small bore, I suppose,' remarked Patrick Campbell.

Sheridan spent most of his life existing on credit, a fact which did not escape his friends or his creditors. After being forced to change homes yet again, he said to one of his associates, Lord Guilford:

'I've just bought a new house. Now everything will go like clock-work.'

'Yes,' said Guilford, 'tick, tick, tick.'

The great eighteenth-century tragedian, John Kemble, was a man of awesome stature and formidable intellect, but he was not a natural singer. One day when he was rehearsing a song, the conductor, who was growing steadily more infuriated by his inability to stay with the accompaniment, finally crashed his baton down on the music-stand and screamed:

'Mr Kemble, you are murdering the time!'

'Sir,' Kemble answered gravely, 'it is better to kill it outright, than to be like yourself, continually beating it.'

Kemble's contemporary, the Scottish barrister Thomas Erskine, who enjoys an unrivalled reputation in the legal world, held the same sway over a court of law as Kemble held over an audience. He was engaged in a case of breach of warranty, in which a horse, declared to be fit, had proved to be completely lame. One of the witnesses had tried to prove the point by claiming that the horse had a cataract in its eye. 'A singular proof of lameness,' said Erskine, 'for what is a "cataract" but a fall?'

Puns which make people look foolish, like Erskine's, are powerful weapons against political opponents. I remember hearing a lovely example of this from an election campaign before the war. A socialist candidate, a Mrs Paling, was speaking at one of her meetings, when she referred to her Tory challenger as a 'dirty dog'. No sooner had she said this, than a voice called out from the floor: 'That's as may be, but we all know what dirty dogs do to palings.'

Even Edward Heath has been known to struggle with an acceptable pun now and again. From the Opposition Front Bench he once attacked the Minister of Transport: 'He has done absolutely nothing to alleviate our traffic problems, but he is the only Minister who produces jam today as well as promising jam tomorrow.'

One of the most amusing puns that I know does not have much to do with acid drops, but it is an example of the sort of wit that's needed to create them. Peter Cook's version of *The Hound of the Baskervilles*, in which he played Sherlock Holmes, included a séance where an anguished spiritualist complained: 'I've lost my spectral guide. She was a medium rare, when the stakes were high.'

Lord Darling was a judge whose own wit was tempered by a sketchy familiarity with everyday life. Enquiring of one barrister, 'And who is George Robey?' he was told, 'He is the Darling of the music halls, my lord.'

In the course of another trial reference was made to the Coliseum, which led Darling to ask:

'Isn't that the place where the Christians were fed to the lions?'

'I think your lordship must be referring to the Trocadero,' he was told, 'where Lyons feed the Christians.'

Of course, the pun is only an aspect of wordplay. The manipulation of proverbs is another highly amusing method that has always appealed to my sense of humour. When Churchill once attended a ball and saw a handsome young aide dancing with an unprepossessing frump, he asked:

'What's he dancing with her for? He's a very good-looking boy', and when it was explained that the aide did not care for women and was only dancing with her for the sake of appearances, Churchill remarked:

'Ah, well, buggers can't be choosers.'

Lines from certain plays have entered the language and gained almost proverbial status. *Hamlet* has a particular distinction in this respect, and the soliloquy 'To be or not to be' contains some of the most famous lines ever written. Oscar Wilde used to parody one of them, turning it into a perceptive aphorism: 'Conscience makes egotists of us all.' And a latter-day reconstruction, reading, 'Thus conscience doth make Noëls of us all', would surely have the Master nodding his approval in the Elysian fields.

Wilde was always playing with words, often at the expense of others. After returning from a visit to America he was asked by a friend about a famous Bostonian hostess, and replied: 'She tried to start a salon, but only succeeded in opening a saloon.'

The renowned eighteenth-century statesman and philosopher, Edmund Burke, may not have shown the same intrinsic wit as Oscar Wilde, but he could manipulate words to achieve the same polemic force. He commented once on kingship: 'Strip "majesty" of its exteriors [first and last letters] and it becomes "a jest".'

The Victorian scholar, William Whewell, was almost as diverse in his scholarship as Burke. Professor of Mineralogy and Professor of Moral Theology at Cambridge within the space of only six years, he aroused the envy of many contemporaries. When an admiring friend told Sydney Smith that Whewell's forte was science, Smith answered: 'Yes, and his foible is omniscience.'

Not surprisingly, Johnson's experience with his dictionary lent him a peculiar virtuosity when it came to playing with words. After reading a manuscript from an aspiring writer, he returned it to the man with the comment: 'Your manuscript is both good and original; but the part that is good is not original, and the part that is original is not good.'

In conversation, the inversion or rearrangement of what other people say can be wickedly amusing, too. Whistler took a special delight in his skill at doing this. He had this mischievous exchange with one of his pupils one day.

'From New York?'

'Yes.'

'Pupil of Chase?'

'Yes.'

'Yes. I thought so. Why did you paint a red elbow with green shadows?'

'I am sure I just paint what I see.'

'Yes. But the shock will come when you see what you paint.'

After entering Parliament, F. E. Smith quickly established a reputation for being a brilliant public speaker, but he could be just as amusing and sharp in his informal speech, too, especially if it presented him with the opportunity of getting the better of the other side. The Labour MP Jimmy Thomas, who was well known for dropping his H's, said to F. E. one day that he had an "orrible 'eadache'. 'You poor fellow,' F. E. commiserated. 'What you need is a couple of aspirates.'

Puns on people's names can't usually be described as acid drops, though I once met a man called Mr Balls who had christened his daughter after Hamlet's lady friend. He delighted to introduce her saying, 'This is my daughter, Ophelia Balls,' and his guests' embarrassment caused him enormous merriment.

Then there is the story of the time when Syngman Rhee was the President of Korea and his brother secured a post with *Time/Life* Magazine. A visitor came into his office one day and cried out: 'Ah sweet Mr Rhee of *Life*, at last I've found you!'

When Winston Churchill was discussing a recently-arrived MP at Westminster, he was told that the man's name was Bossom. 'Bossom? Bossom? What an extraordinary name,' he remarked. 'Neither one thing nor the other.'

In a similar context, Sir Thomas Beecham asked a new member of an orchestra what his name was:
  'Ball, sir.'
  'How very singular.'

Maurice Chevalier was an early enthusiast of 'nouvelle cuisine', before the term was generally applied to exquisitely prepared, but minuscule portions of food. Most of his guests accepted his hospitality without comment, but not the novelist Jacqueline Susann. After dinner with Chevalier, she and her husband were invited to join their host in his study for a glass of brandy. Thanking him, but declining the offer, she explained, 'Maurice, I never drink on an empty stomach.'

Xenophobia

Burning his bed to catch a flea

One of the best ways of putting people down on a general level is the use of xenophobia. In times of crisis or national decline, there is nothing better than a forthright, determined propaganda campaign against another country and its inhabitants. Sixty years ago we were all taught to hate the Germans and love the Russians. Not long afterwards the situation was reversed.

If I was given the opportunity of adopting a second nationality, I would choose German because I admire Teutonic diligence and thoroughness. Historically speaking, it is only comparatively recently that the Bavarians, the Prussians, the Hessians and the rest, sharing only a language, came together to form the Germany we know today. The miracle of their post-war economic recovery owes much to the stability created by figures like Adenauer and Erhard. It is a part of Europe that has always produced and admired strong leadership. The converse arguments would say, 'Yes, it has also produced Frederick the Great and Hitler.' But tyrants have appeared in all countries without diminishing cultural achievement. Look at what the Medicis encouraged, and the Athenians didn't do too badly under Pericles.

Without the historical perspective, popular propaganda of the day ensures that we'll find something derogatory to say about any nation, especially if it was only founded two hundred years ago. America has been the particular butt of xenophobic acid drops. Mentioning this to Peter Cook I once said, 'There are loads of English actors in America,' and Peter said, 'Yes, Dudley Moore spends half his time in California. He's got this thing about space. The Californians have got loads of space – most of it between their ears.'

Criticising the United States is nothing new, of course. In the eighteenth century, Johnson was inveighing against them: 'I am willing to love all mankind, except an American.' In the nineteenth century, Oscar Wilde remarked that: 'America is one long expectoration.' And in another remark, he observed sarcastically: 'America had often been discovered before Columbus, but it had always been hushed up.'

Mark Twain made a similar assessment of his homeland: 'It was wonderful to find America, but it would have been more wonderful to miss it.'

The novelist Anthony Trollope said of his first visit to America: 'In the first place, there is nothing to see, and in the second place, there is no mode of getting about to see anything.'

Of the American himself even harsher criticisms have been made. Bernard Shaw once said: 'The hundred per cent American is ninety-nine per cent idiot.'

And Rudyard Kipling evidently spoke from personal experience when he said: 'The American has no language. He has dialect, slang, provincialism, accent, and so forth.'

Charles Dickens, who had some pretty harsh things to say about the New World in *Martin Chuzzlewit*, wrote: 'Their demeanour is invariably morose, sullen, clownish and repulsive. I should think there is not on the face of the earth a people so entirely destitute of humour, vivacity, or the capacity of enjoyment.'

Thomas Appleton once wrote:

'Good Americans, when they die, go to Paris.'

Oscar Wilde added:

'And when bad Americans die they go to America.'

The English, however, have not been without criticism over the centuries. There is an old Turkish proverb that states: 'An Englishman will burn his bed to catch a flea.'

The German poet, Heinrich Heine, defined silence once as a 'conversation with an Englishman', and Goethe wrote: 'It is related of an Englishman that he hanged himself to avoid the daily task of dressing and undressing.'

When Mark Twain was visiting England he stayed with the owner of an ancient house who took immoderate pride in his family history. As he gave his guest a conducted tour, he paused in front of a picture of the trial of Charles I, pointed to an obscure clerk in the background and said, 'An ancestor of mine.'

Pointing to one of the trial judges, Mark Twain replied, 'An ancestor of mine. But it is no matter, I have others.'

● ● ●

In former East Germany, according to one newspaper, there was even an approved list of abusive terms that were to be applied to the English. These choice pieces of invective ran along the lines:

'Paralytic sycophants, effete betrayers of humanity, carrion-eating servile imitators, arch cowards and collaborators, gang of women-murderers, degenerate rabble, parasitic traditionalists, playboy soldiers and conceited dandies.'

● ● ●

The French and the English have never hit it off. Mutual suspicion and incompatibility have always transformed the *entente cordiale* into angostura bitters. Stendhal said: 'The English are, I think, the most obtuse and barbarous people in the world.' Napoleon thought the English unreliable and complained: 'The English have no exalted sentiments. They can all be bought.'

While President Pompidou once commented: 'The British have three qualities: humour, tenacity and realism. I sometimes think we are still at the humour stage.'

Since many of the great British wits have been Celts, they've been free to use their sardonic talents at the expense of the English to the same extent as their continental counterparts. Oscar Wilde would lampoon the English with impunity, while priding himself on his English urbanity: 'If one could only teach the English how to talk and the Irish how to listen, society would be quite civilised.'

His fellow Irishman, Bernard Shaw, used to say: 'There is nothing so bad or so good that you will not find Englishmen doing it; but you will never find an Englishman in the wrong. He does everything on principle. He fights you on patriotic principles; he robs you on business principles; he enslaves you on imperial principles.'

Opinions about the Scots have sometimes been harsh. Someone once tried to answer Dr Johnson's assertion that Scotland was a vile country, by pointing out that God had made Scotland. Johnson replied: 'Yes, sir. He also made hell.' He also claimed: 'Much may be made of a Scotchman, if he be caught young.'

And Sydney Smith, who spent several years working in Edinburgh, wrote bitterly: 'It requires a surgical operation to get a joke well into a Scotch understanding.'

My own memories of Scotland are affectionate ones. It has provided the theatre with the talents of Alastair Sim and Duncan Macrae, both of whom gave me inordinate pleasure, and from Scotland, too, came Stanley Baxter, a marvellous companion, who once spoke of comedy as 'the channelling of a private misery' – and there is ample evidence of the truth of that in many of the entries recorded here.

Yahoo

G.B.S. – 'idol of thwarted females'

Yahoo

The word Yahoo was invented by one of the greatest English-speaking satirists, Jonathan Swift, to describe a brute in human form. At some time in our lives we have all seen Yahoos, even if they've become tolerably human later on.

Queen Victoria knew all about them, especially after Prince Albert died. Not long after immersing herself in deep mourning, the Widow of Windsor was offered some words of reassurance by the wife of Benjamin Disraeli, who suggested that the Queen's eldest son (the future Edward VII) must be a great comfort to his mother at this sad time.

'Comfort!' retorted the Queen. 'Why, I caught him smoking a fortnight after his father died.'

Bernard Shaw was anathema to many members of the Edwardian establishment, and his self-satisfaction, and self-appointed status as a dissident, provoked the wrath of many critics. These are only a few of the choice comments that were made about Shaw by his fiercest adversaries:

'An idiot child screaming in a hospital' – *H. G. Wells*.

'A desiccated bourgeois, a fossilised chauvinist, a self-satisfied Englishman' – *Pravda*.

'George Bernard Shaw, most poisonous of all the poisonous haters of England; despiser, distorter and denier of the plain truths whereby men live; topsy-turvy perverter of all human relationships; a menace to ordered social thought and ordered social life; irresponsible braggart, blaring self-trumpeter; idol of opaque intellectuals and thwarted females; calculus of contrariwise; flipperty gibbet Pope of chaos; portent and epitome of this generation's moral and spiritual disorder' – *Henry Arthur Jones*.

Sir James Barrie met Shaw in the street one day and told him: 'Shaw, you ought to be roasted alive; though even then, you would not be to my taste.'

Barrie had an unsatisfactory encounter when he met A. E. Housman for the first time. They dined together in Cambridge and though Barrie had been much looking forward to the occasion, the two of them found little to say to each other. At home, Barrie brooded about the disappointing outcome and wrote a note of apology which read:

'Dear Professor Houseman,

I am sorry about last night, when I sat next to you and did not say a word. You must have thought I was a very rude man: I am really a very shy man.

Sincerely yours,

J. M. Barrie.'

Back came Housman's reply:

'Dear Sir James Barrie,

I am sorry about last night, when I sat next to you and did not say a word. You must have thought I was a very rude man: I am really a very shy man.

Sincerely yours,

A. E. Housman.

P. S. And now you have made it worse for you have spelt my name wrong.'

• • •

Mix-ups over names can be deeply humiliating for all concerned. Witness the case of Thor Heyerdahl, the intrepid sailor and anthropologist, who found himself in great demand when he visited London after one of his celebrated voyages. Television companies were

eager to interview him and ITV got in first. Not to be left out, the BBC
arranged for a taxi to collect him from the ITV studio, to speed him to the
Television Centre in time for their broadcast. All went to plan until
Heyerdahl reached the lobby after his first interview and began looking
for his taxi. Several minutes passed, with no sign of his lift, and anxious
about the time, he approached a man in a flat cap who looked as if he
might have been a taxi-driver.

'I'm Thor Heyerdahl,' said the explorer. 'Are you waiting for me?'

'No, mate,' answered the taxi-driver. 'They've sent me to pick up four
Airedales for the BBC.'

• • •

I can sympathise with Shaw. He had an unshaken belief in the importance of working as a social commentator and critic in order, as he
put it, 'to illuminate the dark places of the mind'. His aim was to
enlighten and, in another sphere, I recall Marty Feldman saying much
the same thing about the comedy he was writing in *Round the Horne*.

He'd created some extraordinary characters for me to perform, including one flamboyant extrovert who approached Kenneth Horne with the line, 'Oh, yes, we must brighten up your patio, shove a couple of creepers up your trellis', and generally behaved outrageously. Audiences laughed, but there was some critical disapproval from those who objected to popularising 'high camp'. Marty was unabashed. He told me:

'Even if we do arouse hostility it is much more important to familiarise the public with the outlandish and the uninhibited. Otherwise it is like a ghost in a dark room, and because it is mysterious, people are afraid. We'll turn the light on, let them see what's in the room. Once they've laughed at the spectre they'll no longer be afraid.' He was proved right. The Sixties was a period which made acceptable a whole area of comedy hitherto taboo and unexplored.

It was exactly the same with the Joe Orton plays. In the Sixties, when I was performing his work, there was a lot of anti-Orton feeling, but by the Seventies, the plays were enjoying resounding success. We've come a long way from the time when the Lord Chamberlain refused to let him have an actor playing a policeman say, 'You're *fucking* nicked, my old beauty.' He was told, 'Change it to *bloomin'*, but Joe insisted that the expletive was essential in this context. His script wasn't littered with obscenity and when the rude word came, its impact was all the greater. It reminded me of the shock I got as a young man seeing *Pygmalion* for the first time. When Eliza said 'Not bloody likely', it was like an explosion precisely because of the context. What made the line so successful was its juxtaposition with the formal dialogue of an English tea-party.

Shaw parried his critics, using their own weapons. In some respects his view of man was very like Swift's. If he was ever described as a Yahoo himself, he was perfectly capable of returning the abuse. In one memorable outburst, he attacked the bacteriologist, Dr Edward Bach, over 'monkey gland' treatments and denounced brutality at the same time. He made his opinion of the human race crystal clear:

'Has any ape ever torn the glands from a living man to graft them upon another ape for the sake of a brief and unnatural extension of that ape's life? Was Torquemada an ape? Were the Inquisition and the Star Chamber monkey-houses? Has it been necessary to found a Society for the Protection of ape children, as it has been for the protection of human children? Was the late war of apes or men? Was poison gas a simian or human invention? How can Dr Bach mention the word cruelty in the presence of an ape without blushing? Man remains what he has always been: the cruellest of all animals, and the most elaborately and fiendishly sensual.'

James Joyce was another crusading artist who came in for highly abusive personal criticism after the publication of *Ulysses*. Virginia Woolf described the novel as: 'The work of a queasy undergraduate scratching his pimples.' D. H. Lawrence wrote: 'The last part of it is the dirtiest, most indecent, most obscene thing ever written. It is filthy.'

Lawrence's comments on Joyce himself were even harsher:
'My God, what a clumsy *olla putrida* James Joyce is! Nothing but old fags and cabbage-stumps of quotations from the Bible and the rest, stewed in the juice of deliberate, journalistic dirty-mindedness.'

One of the most effective ways of describing an adversary as a Yahoo is by comparison with one of the great Yahoos of the past. Consider Napoleon Bonaparte or Oliver Cromwell. Both were seen as great men by some, while others viewed them as tyrannical villains. 'Why should Cromwell's statue be erected outside the Houses of Parliament?' one might reasonably ask. Most of the time he ruled without one.

Napoleon falls into the same category. His description of women as little better than breeding machines shows him in his true Yahoo colours:

'Nature intended women to be our slaves. They are our property; we are not theirs. They belong to us, just as a tree that bears fruit belongs to a gardener. What a mad idea to demand equality for women! Women are nothing but machines for producing children.'

Frederick the Great was just as much a tyrannical Yahoo as Napoleon. When he was on his deathbed he asked his physician, Zimmerman, who was treating his final illness:

'You have, I presume, sir, helped many a man into another world.'

'Not so many as Your Majesty,' answered the physician, 'nor with so much honour to myself.'

Naturally there are problems attached to invoking despicable figures of the past, as Bishop Burnett found to his cost in a conversation with the irascible Sarah Churchill, the first Duchess of Marlborough. Burnett, who was famous for his absentmindedness, was talking with the Duchess at dinner on some occasion following her husband's fall from favour with Queen Anne. In the course of their conversation, Burnett compared the Duke to the famous Byzantine general, Belisarius. The Duchess asked him how so great a man could end his days rejected, impoverished and despised by those whom he had served so faithfully. 'Why, madam,' explained Burnett, 'he had such a brimstone of a wife.'

• • •

Anthony Hope, who was no stranger to the Yahoo in fiction after his highly successful 'Ruritanian' romances *Rupert of Hentzau* and *The Prisoner of Zenda*, came out of the opening night of J. M. Barrie's *Peter Pan* and commented: 'Oh for an hour of Herod.'

Critics themselves have always been regarded by writers as a less-than-human species. Rabelais wrote of some long-forgotten critics: 'As for you, little envious prigs, snarling, bastard, puny critics, you'll have railed your last. Go hang yourselves.'

• • •

A few centuries later, Robert Burns launched a similar attack on one of his own critics: 'Thou eunuch of language, thou pimp of gender, murderous accoucheur of infant learning, thou pickle-herring in the puppet show of nonsense.'

To my way of thinking, however, the choicest Yahooing came from President Harry Truman, who read what the music critic of *The Washington Post* had written about a public recital given by his daughter and wrote to the unfortunate individual:

'I have read your lousy review buried in the back pages. You sound like a frustrated old man who never made a success, an eight-ulcer man on a four-ulcer job, and all four ulcers working. I have never met you, but if I do, you'll need a new nose and plenty of beefsteak and perhaps a supporter below.'

Seeing it free on television

Zany

Noël Coward developed a flawless system for getting the better of people whom he met, but whose name he had forgotten, or had never known. People used to ask him:

'How do you manage, because you must always be meeting people who think you should know their names, when of course you don't?'

He would reply: 'Oh yes, I always say to them, "What is your name?" and they say "Frank" or whatever it is, and then I say, "I know your first name as well as I know my own is Noël, I mean your second name." And if they say "Smith" I say, "Well I know you're Smith as well as I know that I'm Coward, I mean what's your first name?"'

After that he would explain:

'I always add ... "And how is Muriel?", which puts them at a complete loss, because they have to think, "Do I know Muriel?"'

The use of zany non sequiturs like this is a marvellous way of unsettling and confounding other people. It throws them off their line of attack and allows us time to prepare for a riposte. Frequently, zany humour of this type is far more amusing than conventional wit. I used to write a lot of my own material, and I remember once writing about someone who was short-sighted. I went on and on about it, saying things like: 'You have to take him up to Big Ben and let him feel the hands.' I remember thinking it was quite funny at that time, but I was not sure, so I embellished it with other gags. But in the event it was that line which got more laughs than anything else.

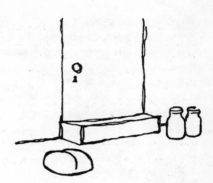

•••

Some equally zany dialogue occurred when I was filming with Fenella Fielding. We were both squeezed into a little gig for a shot of the two of us riding along. The seat was tiny, and we were crushed together for the close-up. Suddenly Fenella asked: 'Why is your bum so hard, do you leave it out at night?' This kind of surrealism, with its dotty funniness, will always light up any conversation.

•••

Marty Feldman had the same ability to refashion a well-known phrase. He once wrote: 'It had been in the family for years and years handed down from generation to generation – until the handle dropped off.'

Zany non sequiturs or descents into bathos are perfect for ridiculing and deflating the over-serious or persistently annoying. Oscar Wilde, escorting an over-earnest lady into dinner, was told by her:

'What terrible weather we are having.'

'Yes, but if it wasn't for the snow, how could we believe in the immortality of the soul?' Wilde remarked.

'What an interesting question, Mr Wilde. But tell me exactly what you mean?'

'I haven't the slightest idea.'

The eminent Jesuit, Archbishop Roberts, was once asked by an interviewer whether he had ever experienced any doubts about his vocation. When he answered that he had, the man asked him earnestly:

'Well, what kept you in the Society?'
'Muffins on Thursdays.'

The Revd Sydney Smith paid a call on a fellow writer in Edinburgh and found to his astonishment that the man was poring over a book that he was supposed to be reviewing. Smith asked the man why he was reading it, and his friend replied by asking him exactly how else he was to perform the critical task?

'Oh, I never read a book before reviewing it,' Smith replied. 'It prejudices a man so.'

The originator of spoonerisms, the Revd Dr Spooner, came face to face with a student whom he had taught several years earlier at New College.

'Good evening, Dr Spooner. I don't suppose you remember me. My name is...', started the ex-student.

'On the contrary,' interjected Spooner, 'I remember your name perfectly, but I must admit that I've completely forgotten your face.'

Owning, running and more often than not taking the lead at Her Majesty's Theatre meant that Beerbohm Tree invariably had a lot on his mind as he prepared for a performance. One evening he was called from his dressing-room as he was making up as Svengali and hurried down to the stage with a huge black beard and a massive wig of mad, dark hair. There was someone waiting to see him at the stage-door, but Tree, preoccupied, brushed past him without a word and then came scuttling back full of apologies and explaining, 'My dear fellow, I'm so sorry. I didn't recognize you in my beard.'

There is a lovely story about Donald Wolfit which fits into this category. He was performing *Lear* at the King's Theatre, Hammersmith, and had asked Ellen Pollock to play Regan. During the rehearsals she went to the wardrobe to try on the Regan costume that had been worn by successive actresses for the last fifteen years. It was clear, however, that the costume was the wrong size for her, and she went along to Wolfit's dressing-room wearing it to complain to him that it did not fit. 'That's funny,' he commented, 'it always used to fit.'

The critical jibes between one artist and another are seldom intended to benefit the object of criticism, but there was a charming incident during the reign of Charles I when this was the case. The poet George Withers was imprisoned for his 'Abuses, Stript and Whipt', and together with other charges he faced a death penalty. However, his fellow poet Sir John Denham appealed to the King for clemency by claiming: 'If Your Majesty kills Withers, I will then be the worst poet in England.' And the King relented.

Groucho Marx is one of my own favourite zany comics. Apart from the many wonderful remarks attributed to him in real life, my favourite Marxism comes from *A Night in Casablanca*. Groucho is behind the desk in a hotel reception when a man comes in with this huge woman and says that he wishes to register.

'You've no reservation. Who are you?' asks Groucho.

'I'm Mr Smith.'

'A likely story.'

'I *am* Mr Smith – and this is Mrs Smith, my wife.'

'She's your *wife*?'

'Of course, she's my wife. You should be ashamed of yourself.'

'If she's your wife, *you* should be ashamed of yourself.'

Apart from the stars, though, the great movie moguls and directors have their own brand of peculiar humour. While we were playing in *Captain Brassbound's Conversion*, Ingrid Bergman invited me to dinner with her friend, Alfred Hitchcock. The great man was rather annoyed because none of the films in which he had directed her were listed in

the programme. But during the meal he started talking about filming of
The Birds:

'I had all these birds on the set behind chicken wire, hundreds of
birds, and I had the camera and everything ready. Then Jessica Tandy
came on the set; all these birds were going to fly at her at the appropriate moment, but when she saw the birds behind the chicken wire, she
became very frightened, apprehensively holding down her skirt. So I
went up to her and told her, "Don't worry, Jessica, remember the old
saying A Bird in the Hand..."'

He didn't have to finish it, we were all laughing except Ingrid, who
asked what was so funny.

Alfred turned to me despairingly: 'It's no good telling jokes to
foreigners.'

Someone told me a story about Walt Disney watching some of the
rushes from *Fantasia* in which all the centaurs were galloping about in
time to Beethoven's Pastoral Symphony. After they had finished, the
great animator turned to one of his crew and exclaimed: 'Gee! This will
make Beethoven!'

Probably the best-known movie mogul in this respect is Sam
Goldwyn. Whether or not he actually said all the lines attributed to
him, he must have said one or two very like them in order to establish
the reputation in the first place. These are some of the most amusing
Goldwynisms:

'Who wants to go out and see a bad movie when they can stay at
home and see it free on television?'

'There'd be a great improvement if they shot less film and more
producers.'

'A verbal contract isn't worth the paper it's written on.'

'The reason so many people turned up at Louis Mayer's funeral was
because they wanted to make sure he was dead.'

'If you can't give me your word of honour, will you give me your
promise?'

'Anyone who goes to see a psychiatrist needs his head examined.'

Hearing the news that his son had become engaged, Goldwyn reputedly told a newspaper reporter: 'Thank heavens. A bachelor's life is no life for a single man!'

Dorothy Parker found herself living again as a single woman, when her husband, Alan Campbell, died. Among the small crowd gathered to watch his body being taken from the house was a neighbour who had liked him, pretended to like his wife and who always enjoyed meddling in other people's troubles.

'Dottie – tell me, dear, what I can do for you,' she asked as the hearse drove away.

'Get me a new husband,' was Dorothy Parker's answer.

After a brief silence, but before anyone who might have laughed did laugh, her neighbour said, 'I think that is the most callous and disgusting remark I ever heard in my life.'

'So sorry,' replied Dorothy Parker, adding gently, 'Run down to the corner and get me a ham and cheese on rye and tell them to hold the mayo.'

The final zany word must go however to the American murderer, James Rodgers, who, facing his firing squad, was asked whether he had any last request and replied: 'Why, yes! A bullet-proof vest.'

Behind that wisecracking wish for armour lies the desire to avoid the inevitable, to cheat drowsy death and have life a little longer. Many of us sometimes imagine that such a feeling is universal, but there are exceptions: Schopenhauer said of existence, 'I would willingly have changed it for a never-having-been' and Wilde assures us that 'All trials are trials for one's life.' The real reward of adversity is what we learn in overcoming it. Humour is a great mainstay in misfortune, but we mustn't take the funny maxim too literally on the way. 'Laugh and the world laughs with you' is impractical advice to a mourner, and you shouldn't tell an ex-alcoholic in a brewery, 'A little of what you fancy does you good.' Lines like 'The best things in life are free' may suit lyric writers, but they'll elicit a raspberry from an undischarged bankrupt. The quote, like opportunity, like food and indeed like love, has got to come at the right moment, then it will fly like an arrow to its target and they'll cry, as in *Hamlet*, 'A hit, a hit, a palpable hit!' But blurted out without proper consideration it can send your ego round your ankles and leave you feeling as hapless as the man who sang, 'When your hair has turned to silver...' to the platinum blonde who retorted, 'I will go and pawn my head.'